# CHILDREN, WHAT ARE THEY?

E. C. M. Frijling-Schreuder

translated by
Katherine Stechmann

INTERNATIONAL UNIVERSITIES PRESS, INC.

*New York*

Manufactured in the United States of America

# CONTENTS

# 1  EARLY DEVELOPMENT

*Why do people have children?*

Now that contraception is a simple matter and is almost universally practiced, we might assume that most pregnancies are voluntary and that normally a woman would not become pregnant without wanting to. But such a simplistic view is very misleading. What is meant by "wanting"? And from what motives do people want to have children? Only a fraction of these motives are conscious; mostly, they are unconscious.

The mother's emotional attitude toward the expected child is similarly determined by a number of conscious and unconscious factors.

What is normal covers a wide field between the abnormal and the optimal (Deutsch, 1944). The ideal situation is perhaps the one in which a young married couple decide jointly that they want to have a child. But such motives as, "I want to have a baby before my younger girl friend does" may also be normal. Many a child is born out of the motive, "If I'm pregnant, he'll surely marry me," or is conceived as the result of a careless whim or of an aversion to contraception. And sometimes a protest against the parents or disappointment in them may be the unconscious motive for an involuntary pregnancy in an adolescent.

This does not mean that the pregnancy should be interrupted or that a normal bond between mother and child cannot be formed once the baby is born.

*How does a normal mother-child relationship look to a newborn child?*

Who can say? The psychic life of the infant is a fascinating subject for speculation, for the baby cannot contradict anything. And so the birth process has been viewed as the foundation of all later anxiety; and some investigators have ascribed to the infant the most elaborate and involved fantasies.

Setting all this aside, if we look at the way the newborn infant acts, we see nothing remarkable. Breathing begins with a cry, and thereupon the infant—if he is looked after normally—goes to sleep and sleeps for a considerable time (Spitz, 1965). This may be alarming for many young mothers, especially with the first child. To a woman, however sophisticated, birth is a tremendous event, and the complete silence of the baby for hours so soon afterward is totally unexpected.

During the first few days, pride in the baby often alternates with anxiety: "What's wrong? Is he still alive? He's so quiet!"

It is generally known that a mother feels secure about her baby if she has a fairly uncomplicated love for him, and that the more conflicting her emotions are, the more anxious she may feel about him. That is so, but we must not forget that every emotion has some conflict within it, and that some anxiety on the part of the mother during the first few days of her child's life is quite normal.

This applies also to breast feeding, and particularly to the first feeding of the first child, especially if the young mother has her heart set on nursing the baby. If the confinement takes place in a hospital and the baby is brought to her by a busy and perhaps impatient nurse, disappointments may ensue that can be overcome by a normal person, but that still do not promote the development of an optimal mother-child relationship. A mother who receives the proper help with the early feedings finds the adjustment a great deal easier; but here again the margin between the normal and the optimal is a wide one. The same is true of the baby's little discomforts which make an anxious mother uneasy. Slowly and with some uncertainty the normal mother learns to interpret the signals that the normal infant sends out.

The union between mother and child is no longer purely physical, as it was during pregnancy; it is a psychobiological union in which, for the time being, the mother still protects, cares for, and provides warmth and security for the infant. The nature of the mother's love for her baby determines whether she will comprehend the child's primitive signals. This is the first necessity. No mother, however, is wholeheartedly full of love for her baby; and angry impulses toward such a frail little creature may easily engender guilt feelings. These, in turn, cause an inner conflict that uses up energy and disturbs her sensitivity to the signals that the child sends out. She may then become anxious whenever the baby cries and take him up too often. The baby may react by vomiting—if there is a tendency toward this—and naturally this increases the mother's anxiety. General reassurances are of little help in such a situation. The doctor must, together with the mother, patiently work out the best diet for the baby. Then the mother will gradually come to feel that she really knows how to look after her child and will take it less seriously if he cries now and then.

Some mothers, on the other hand, have difficulty in

taking note of the baby's crying. They are afraid of spoiling the baby, or they do not want to be disturbed by him except at times of their own choosing. For the baby this means an excessively high level of unpleasant stimuli, and this disturbs the development of a primary feeling of security.

Spitz (1965) investigated a number of what he called "psychotoxic" mother-child relationships and described how disturbances arise when a hypersensitivity of the child engenders a particular defensive pattern in the mother. In mothers who cannot bear to hear the baby cry this takes the form of oversolicitude. In certain children with eczema, Spitz demonstrated heightened abdominal and cremasteric[1] reflexes which indicated an increased sensitivity to skin stimuli. He noticed too that the mothers of these children warded off their unconscious hostility toward the child by touching him as little as possible. Here again is a vicious circle, for naturally the eczema increases the anxiety about caressing the child

The doctor's most important role is that of giving support and encouragement. For just as a vicious circle may evolve between a mother and a baby with specific oversensitivity, so the mother's feeling of peace and security may help to overcome little constitutional anomalies.

We know very little about what goes on within a young infant. After only a few days the baby turns his head toward the breast when his mother picks him up. After a few weeks he smiles when he sees a human face. Later still, he stops his hunger cries when he hears his

---

[1] The cremasteric is the muscle that draws up the testis.

mother's voice. The baby learns very quickly. At two months he follows his mother's movements with his eyes, and at four months he turns toward sounds. At four months he can hold his head up when he is lying on his stomach, and at seven months he can roll from one side to the other. He plays with his hands and looks with interest at his waggling feet. He can bring his hand to his mouth and put his toys in his mouth. He crows and makes little noises, either spontaneously or in response to his mother's prattle. But there is still a great deal that he does not know. Whether his mother or a stranger smiles at him, he returns the smile with equal generosity.

After the first eight months the baby begins to make a distinction between familiar and strange faces. It is as if he discovered with a shock, "That isn't mother! Where is mother?" And he screams at his grandmother, whose ministrations in feeding and diapering he accepted with great pleasure only a week ago. It is always difficult for grandparents to realize that this is to be expected and that it will pass off as soon as the baby discovers that after the sight of another face his mother is still there too.

At that time the baby starts to carry out what Mahler (1968) calls "customs inspection": he feels a stranger's face, especially the mouth, and he does the same with his mother. He also reconnoiters a bit before he embarks upon the adventure of letting a stranger pick him up and talk to him. In his crib he now slowly pulls himself up and sometimes hangs there exhausted, having apparently forgotten how to go about sitting down again. In his high chair he no longer submits quietly to being settled in but squirms to get out; at the same time, he has no understanding of a situation and no concept of danger. While being fed he bangs his hands into his cereal with great enthusiasm, or plops the spinach into his mother's face. Mothers react very differently to this sort of thing. Perhaps this is the place to point out that a baby does not have the same mother at all times: mothers are changeable in mood, they have their own problems and their own interests aside from the baby, whereas the baby is completely dependent on the mother. Moreover, each stage of life has a different significance in the mother's emotions.

A young woman who has derived intense enjoyment from the little being who grew within her and who lay in her arms, complete and rosy, may find it very difficult when the child begins to develop his own independence and manifests this in primitive and extremely trouble-some ways.

Sometimes a young mother who found the baby an encumbrance and bathing him almost too great a respon-sibility may particularly enjoy watching her child as he sturdily pulls himself up by her hands and, supporting himself on her knees, jumps up at her.

The first mother may perhaps try to restrain the incipient independence by leaving the child in the crib too long or by wanting to nurse him too long. It may also happen that a young woman who has a great need for a baby that she can cuddle reacts to the beginnings of independence by feeling offended and turning away from the child, and is unable to give the child the intensive care of which he is still in great need. In most mothers all three of these emotional currents are blended. Mahler (1968) describes excellently not only how the mother learns to understand her child as an individual, but also how the child makes use of the guidelines that the mother offers him.

Whether a mother enjoys letting her child run and jump, is tolerant when he creeps along the ground, and can effectively protect him against serious dangers, or whether, on the other hand, she has great need of a passive baby and sings and talks to him a great deal, will lead to different character formations, but both babies may develop quite normally. As for the other factors that determine character formation—the defenses, the Oedipus complex, latency—I shall take these up in later chapters.

## Handling stimuli and the rise of awareness

In contrast to what was formerly assumed, the observations of Spitz (1965) show that the stimulus threshold of infants is usually high. Exceptions occur, and these constitute a danger to normal development. Among the first perceptions of the child, those which predominate are not sight and hearing, but much more diffuse sensations arising, for example, in the mouth and the abdomen, which do not become conscious in the adult sense.

Another group of perceptions is that of the diffuse touch and proprioceptive sensations originating in changes of position, in being held, being diapered, and so on. Spitz describes brilliantly how perception develops from the diffuse *Gestalt* of the mother's head, which appears above the child in all her dealings with him.

The precise moment at which what Spitz calls "reception"—that is, the reception of stimuli—turns into "perception," or awareness with recollection, cannot be stated exactly. And theoretically it must differ in different children, since the myelinization of the optic nerve and of the higher centers continues after birth. The combination of maturation and adaptation based on a particular degree of maturation results in a wide variation. The gaze the infant fixes on his mother during breast feeding probably represents only a preliminary stage of seeing. However that may be, it is certain that in a six-month-old baby there is already a lively interaction by means of eye contact.

The stimulus threshold for sound is high to begin with. In the case of nervous infants who cry at every sound in the environment one must consider the possibility of a disturbance—for example, a minimal brain dysfunction.

From birth onward, the baby makes himself heard; and the mother quickly concludes that she can interpret the crying. We must remember, however, that her interpretations may be partly prompted by cultural stereotypes (Wolff, 1969). There is some question, for example, whether babies are really uncomfortable when they are wet. But in general it is true that there are very different types of crying. Each mother establishes an interplay with her child regarding the different ways in which these types of crying are answered: by feeding, by diapering, or merely by looking at him.

After about two months the infant begins to listen, and about the third month he himself may begin to vocalize and to notice the sound he makes (Bladergroen, 1966). Very soon this leads, with a normal mother, to an interaction in the form of "making sounds together." It appears that in this process the mother reacts to the stimulus emanating from the child, rather than the reverse. With very quiet children a vicious circle may easily result. It is difficult for a mother to make little sounds to an infant who fails to answer them, so that a disturbance of contact tends to become aggravated. The reverse is also true. The differences in normal temperament in this respect tend to approach the average if the mother does not allow them to upset her (Fries and Woolf, 1953).

Vocalizing, and certainly concerted vocalizing, is a forerunner of speech. I shall offer no opinion on whether this is also true of the various forms of crying. One form of crying, in any case, has a different significance: the desperate crying which continues until the child falls asleep from exhaustion and which indicates that he has been traumatically overwhelmed by internal or external stimuli. Once the child is in this condition, it is difficult for the mother to give the right kind of help. A shrieking infant, for example, cannot react immediately to the stimulus of the nipple in his mouth; thus it takes a great effort to induce suckling in a baby who has been hungry for too long. This is one of the reasons why the system of rigid feeding schedules has been abandoned.

It is not by chance that I chose the example of suckling: the warm milk and the sucking form the first intense satisfaction, which may be observed not only in the beatific smile of the satiated infant but also in the fervor with which infants suck their fingers between feedings.

Emotionally healthy mothers have no trouble with the ardent sucking of the child. Complications occur only if the mother herself cannot endure thumb-sucking, has a need to adhere to a too rigid or otherwise unsuitable feeding system, or is unable to feel sufficient concern for her child. Emotionally healthy mothers regard with tenderness the vehemence with which the baby sucks his thumb. For the development of the incipient consciousness, this thumb-sucking is important. It produces a pleasurable—though perhaps largely unconscious—feeling, and thus promotes the baby's sense of security and stability.

Hoffer (1949) has beautifully illustrated with his films of newborn babies how the infant's mouth is constantly in motion, and he has carefully analyzed how thumb-sucking helps in learning to distinguish between the self and the environment. For how can a baby know that sensations of warmth, softness, and moisture experienced in breast feeding originate in a source in the outer world? Whether he ever "knows" it is, in fact, questionable, for an infant naturally does not think in words. But there are sensations within the mouth and in the entire body that are connected with the feeding situation and that the child himself cannot arouse though they appease his hunger. There are also sensations in the mouth that are coupled with sensations in the thumb, the hand, the arm, and that the child can arouse himself; but they do not interrupt the hunger stimuli. We may insert here another important general observation concerning development: a child who has had sufficient oral gratification as an infant will, in the toddler stage, more easily find age-appropriate gratifications. This early thumb-sucking will then disappear of its own accord.

The observation that full initial gratification helps to advance development is important in all phases. For doctors and dentists, who are often concerned about possible malformations of the jaw resulting from excessive thumb-sucking, it is important to know that if they do not combat the thumb-sucking of an infant they will not, as a rule, need to combat it in the toddler; it will disappear spontaneously.

In his first months the baby has as yet very little occasion to deal with unpleasant stimuli. Stimuli are immediately disposed of; for example, there is as yet no regularity in excretion, a full bladder or colon leading at once to wetting or soiling of the diaper. The stimulus of cold during diaper change causes wetting of the fresh diaper; a fullness in the abdomen as the stomach becomes filled causes soiling while nursing.

The maintenance of an internal balance is accomplished by means of the direct discharge of unpleasant stimuli. The gratification derived from thumb-sucking contributes toward this end by acting as a stabilizing factor. For the removal of unpleasant stimuli the baby is completely dependent on his mother. The baby and the toddler can express disturbances of equilibrium only by physical means. A disturbed mother-child relationship is manifested in the baby by crying, vomiting, nocturnal restlessness, diarrhea, or constipation. When an adult patient expresses psychic conflicts in physical symptoms, we call these conversion symptoms. We can interpret them as a regression to this very early form of removal of tension, although this does not take into account the content of the psychic conflict (Kuiper, personal communication). But we cannot apply the interpretation in reverse. Every infant may have a few days of crying now and then, may vomit occasionally—this is of no consequence.

Furthermore, our culture is not optimal for the maintenance of this primitive stimulus balance, or homeostasis. Our mothers do not carry their babies with them all day, and thus the child does not feel the natural body warmth of his mother all day long. We accustom the child—even if we do not follow a rigid feeding schedule—to a certain regularity in feeding, if only by virtue of the fact that he lies in his crib between feedings. In primitive cultures the baby, constantly carried along, is moved to the breast whenever he wants (Whiting and Child, 1953).

The development of the culture always involves progression and retrogression at the same time. Each step means a lessening of instinctual gratification and thus an increase in vulnerability (Freud, 1929). I shall return to this point from time to time in order to make as clear as possible which factors in our own culture tend to promote psychic vigor and which tend to reduce it.

*The beginnings of independence*

After a few months, looking and vocalizing are augmented by playing with hands and feet and looking at the fingers when they come into the field of vision, whether accidentally or intentionally. After about eight months the passive little creature without muscular co-ordination has become a rather active baby, who can roll himself from one side to the other. He can already take hold of things and sit up by himself, and he is gradually beginning to make efforts to creep. His mother is asking herself, "Can he still be put in the crib? Won't he fall out of the carriage?"

Mothers find the beginning of motor development pleasant but troublesome; it is a fact that the infant is in this period rather a danger to himself. He tries to put his fingers into the wall socket, or to pull himself up to the boiling kettle.

As soon as he can pull himself up to a standing position, he can fall out of the crib or the carriage, and as he creeps across a room, he bumps into things; thus he requires a great deal of watching during this period. It is no wonder that this is the period when mothers complain about being overburdened.

A child of about a year is already an individual. He can creep away from his mother, he recognizes his mother and father, he has his own ideas about what he does and does not want to eat. He is wet at regular times and may even have set times for soiling his diaper. He leaves his mother in no doubt as to what he wants, and among his earliest communications, after "mama," come "yes" and "no," by means of nodding and headshaking or in words (Spitz, 1957).

This process of separation and individuation will continue throughout life, but up to and during the third year it is an extremely important element in development. The mother can let her ten-month-old infant creep by himself while she is present and can watch to see that he does not injure himself. The two-year-old runs babbling around her. The three-year-old remains quietly playing in the room while his mother is busy elsewhere in the house.

The gradually increasing independence also causes problems. Fraiberg (1965) has entered exceptionally well into the creeping infant's world of experience and has given an excellent description of it. This is the time of endless voyages of exploration: every object is an unknown mountaintop. The underside of the chair on which mother is sitting provides an entirely different landscape from that of its armrests and back seen from his mother's arms. The area beneath father's desk is a spacious house where you can make a delightful stay with a soft cuddle-toy. Plants are demolished when the earth needs to be examined or when they are used as supports (usually treacherous ones) in getting up. Everything within reach is inspected.

### The practicing period

Every adult is impressed by the energy that the child displays in these voyages of discovery. It is the age at which one experiences the most. The toddler sees the world by turns in a frog's eyeview, while lying on his stomach, and in grand vistas, when he clings to a table leg or the sofa. An endless variety of stimuli assails him, and for the first time he can actively control them. He explores the stairs, and once he has discovered them he can easily spend an entire day climbing up a stairway which he cannot descend because he has not yet discovered the trick of turning around at the top.

This period of heightened activity is coupled with good humor. Mahler (1968) calls this the "practicing period"; Greenacre (1957), in connection with the childhood of the artist, speaks of "the love affair with the world." While engaged in these discoveries the child is less sensitive to pain than he will later become. He falls, gets up, falls again, climbs up on the sofa, falls off, cries, is picked up and consoled, and climbs up again.

The discovery of the mouth is still important in this period: everything is shoved into his mouth. At the same time his hands explore surfaces, pinch, and grasp. Toys are thrown out of the playpen, and this becomes a particularly fine game when an adult throws them back in, so that the process can be repeated.

One thing is certain: every adult tires of this game before the baby does. Freud (1920) has connected the game with one of the earliest typical ways in which a small child masters difficulties. The active discarding of the toy and its restoration are used as compensation for the passive experience of the disappearance of the mother, who goes out of the room from time to time. This active repetition of a passive experience accompanies us throughout our lives as a means of dealing with difficulties. In childhood it plays an important role.

The constant activity of the one- to two-year-old makes it difficult for him to quiet down, and it is also responsible for the fact that the child's good humor may alternate with listlessness and overfatigue. Difficulties in falling asleep during this time rest upon this constant urge toward activity, but also upon the fact that mother is not there. For, with the possibility of creeping or walking away from his mother, the child continually encounters unexpected situations, in which she is not immediately at hand, and in this phase he needs to have his mother accessible more than at any other time. A closed door is often still an impregnable obstacle and may give rise to frightened screaming. And so being in bed means to the child not only sleeping, but also separation from mother. He does not yet understand that his mother is still there even though he does not see her; he must convince himself, by crying or by climbing out of bed and looking for her, that his mother is still within reach. The mother can make the transition from waking to sleeping easier by ending the day with singing to him and looking at pictures with him.

It is one of the basic misunderstandings between parents and children that the mother, after a day with a child of about a year and a half, is dead tired, and therefore thinks that the youngster must be too. But the child, no matter how exhausted, is always ready for new adventures.

Once the command of motor activity has been achieved, the child quiets down a bit, and his mood becomes less stable.

As I have already said, the unexpected situations that the one-to two-year-old constantly faces may constitute a threat. By this I do not mean primarily the frequent falls and bumps that occur in this phase. As we have seen, he accepts these—so long as his mother does not become anxious. But the very fact of walking causes him to be unexpectedly away from his mother, in situations with which he cannot cope. This also makes it harder for the mother to adjust exactly to his needs, although many young women succeed in this quite spontaneously. One should not be overoptimistic however. Young mothers are often told: "Let him fall; he has to learn," an advice that may confuse them. It is a typical example of global and undifferentiated thinking. Sometimes the child needs to master the falling himself; sometimes he needs to know that mother is there to comfort him. At every moment he falls back on his mother's presence. In this way he refuels, as Furer (Mahler, 1968) expresses it. As soon as he starts to talk, he is seldom silent except when he is asleep. "Mama," "Look, mama," is his watchword for the entire day. Next to the need for warmth and cuddling now comes the need for admiration of his achievements.

# 2　FATHERS

In the description of the child's early development, the father remained in the background. In the psychological mother-infant dyad, the father does not play a direct role. Nevertheless, the husband can give his wife a great deal of support to help her feel secure in her motherhood.

For the husband, expecting and having a child means something entirely different than for the wife. While pregnancy is for a woman often—though not always—a great fulfillment, for a man his wife's pregnancy is often—though not always—a burden, even if he himself really wants the child. And no matter how proud of the baby the new father is, and though he may find it not unpleasant to diaper the baby or give him his bottle, still there is often a feeling, conscious or unconscious, of rivalry with the baby who takes up so much of his wife's attention and interest.

When a couple decide to have a child—even when the decision has been made by the two together—the pregnancy, birth, and nursing period represents entirely different experiences for the two parents. It is just this difference in experience that leads emotionally healthy people to further grow in adulthood. On the other hand, the neurotic interaction in a disturbed marriage may take an unfavorable turn as a result of it. In the most unfavorable case the jealousy leads to revenge reactions on the part of the husband—neglect of his wife, possibly unfaithfulness. It is clear that it then becomes almost impossible for a woman to feel secure toward her child.

Equally the wife, if she cannot completely enter into her husband's feelings during this period, may endanger the mutual relationship.

Tension in a pregnant woman or disturbances in the mother-child relationship in the first few months of the baby's life may very well be based on neurotic interaction in the marriage, stemming from the father (Frijling-Schreuder, 1965a). Conversely, the mother can enjoy her child without constraint to the degree that the father is able to enjoy his family. Sometimes he is mellowed by mother and child together; sometimes he himself may also, from the beginning, be proud of the baby and enjoy helping with caring for him.

Just once I saw a clear competition arise between father and mother over the care of the baby, in which the father more or less pushed the mother aside, or at least observed her with such caviling criticism that the spontaneous mother-child relationship was thereby also disturbed. But such a reaction on the part of a man to the birth of his child no longer falls within normal limits, even though it is culturally encouraged by today's leveling tendencies in the man-woman relationship. The advantage of this cultural displacement is, however, that in a normal relationship the father takes an active part in the baby's care and derives unrestrained enjoyment from him.

In his second half-year the baby also has, for his own part, a definite relationship with his father. He then undoubtedly experiences his father as a trusted person, is willing to play on his lap, to pull himself up by his fingers, and later, when he begins to stand, to use his father's legs as supports. He has his own little sound of pleasure when his father comes home, his firm expectation of being picked up and cuddled. Romping with his father soon becomes a standing delight, passive at first, but later quite active on the baby's part as he takes possession of his father by drumming on his chest with his fists. The bond with the father thus has its own nuances from the very start.

The horseplay that fathers so gladly engage in may, if it does not take place in optimal fashion, easily give rise to a multitude of stimuli that the child cannot master; then the romp ends in crying. But if it goes well, it helps to overcome fear, since some fear is always aroused, which is then dispelled in play. In that respect it is a precursor of the later practice of sports. To indulge in acrobatics with a powerful father also produces a feeling of power, especially if the stunts are at the same time entirely safe, so that the child really does not hurt himself and the fear has only the intensity of a pleasant suspense. Then the child-father unit becomes omnipotent, and the child's experience of these prideful feelings of power is a primitive precursor of the later confidence that constitutes the basis of the ego ideal.

Like the mother, the father is a powerful source of help, a kind fortifier of the child's developing personality, someone who picks you up when you have fallen, who solves insoluble problems, such as heavy doors or loose joints in toys, whose presence brings security.

What has the toddler of fifteen to eighteen months achieved up to now? He can see and hear. He understands simple language, though his own active use of language is still limited. He is to a great extent master of his movements, can push little sticks into openings, can run or creep toward a toy. He can name his father and mother and distinguish them from strangers. His bond with them has altered from a passive to an active one. He possesses them literally: he climbs onto their laps and scrambles down again.

Although many infants of this age are sensitive to tension in their parents and most mothers know from their own observation that children are particularly difficult when their mother is out of sorts, this very observation indicates that parents, from the infant's point of view, have no personality of their own and possess no rights. The parents are there for him, not he for them; and in that respect there is not yet a true reciprocity in the relationship. This reciprocity does exist in a primitive form: a well-cared-for child, loved by his parents, gives himself to them in full trust and pleasure. However, it is not only in language that the distinction between "I" and "you" is delayed until a later stage. For some time to come the child will very gradually detach himself from the early mother-child unit; and the more gradually this process advances and the fewer the shocks involved, the more firmly established the later independence will be

The difference between generations is at present so greatly emphasized that it is not superfluous to note that there are many parents who enjoy their children and that they have a perfect right to do so. The more pleasure they take in their children, the more pleasure and trust the children have in them—and thus in their entire lives. The parents are the child's first reality. The way in which they experience their child forms an important basis for the child's self-confidence. His world broadens out slowly, and his adjustment to the outer world begins to develop in these early years in accordance with the expectations that his parents arouse in him through their attitudes.

# 3 THE DEVELOPMENT OF DRIVES AND OF EMOTIONAL TIES IN THE FIRST EIGHTEEN MONTHS

A screaming infant may appear to be desperate, but also furious, and his mother asks comfortingly, "What's my baby so mad about?" She at least is certain that she recognizes rage in the crying. When the baby is nursing or sucking his fingers, she is even more certain that this is pleasurable to him.

On the basis of these and other observations on children and of observations in the analysis of adults, we assume that from birth onward two instinctual drives manifest themselves, each of which has its own development: aggression and the libido. Drives are in themselves not observable; their energy is expended in impulses that may or may not lead to action. In adult life they enter the consciousness as wishes, emotions, and fantasies: sexual wishes, hostile wishes, emotions of hate or love. These wishes are considered, assessed; feeling and thought estimate the consequences of translating the impulses into action. Thought and feeling set themselves up as testing stations between the drive impulse and its expression

The great convertibility of the drives makes it possible for their energy to be used in a great many activities. In the early months of live there is little evidence of this process. We have seen how at that time every stimulus leads to its discharge. The furiously crying infant tosses his arms about, and may in the process scratch his own face. The infant who has just been fed is a very model of satiety. Quite soon he progresses a little way: an infant who is not extremely hungry may be quieted by the sound of his mother's voice.

At what precise moment rage becomes coupled with a feeling of rage is hard to say. Certainly one can see in a fifteen-month-old how pleasurable a discharge of rage can be. He screams, throws himself on the floor, pounds on the floor with hands and feet. During the outburst itself this produces a wonderful feeling of power, and at first it does not leave a hangover, as it does in the case of an adult.

We have seen that the infant soon learns to stop crying for a moment when he hears his mother's voice. That means, in addition to the beginnings of tolerance of unpleasure, also a first attempt at delaying pleasure. Instinctual stimuli do not, in principle, tolerate much delay. At the beginning every hunger stimulus demands immediate satisfaction: feeding. If there is no satisfaction, discomfort sets in and is discharged in crying. When the infant quiets down on hearing his mother's voice or seeing her face and her movements, he has taken a significant step in his development. The immediate gratification of a drive by means of feeding is postponed, and energy is thereby made available for seeing and hearing the mother, who provides the feeding. This becomes a precursor both of recognition of the mother and of loving her. From the very beginning an infant clutches a finger that touches the palm of his hand, and after a few months he also tries to grasp things within his reach, including his mother's breast. Many infants knead the breast with their hands—a precursor of that possession which we have already discussed in connection with horseplay. Slowly, sucking is joined by biting, which also is a more active taking into possession.

The aggressive energy that could be released only in crying and pounding can now be directed toward someone. This is now made clear to the mother in other ways as well—the baby of seven or eight months can actively resist and be very cross when his diaper is being changed. At about a year this active resistance is joined by negative headshaking and later by saying "no." At the same time wetting and soiling the diaper changes from something that merely happens to something more active and pleasurable. A child of this age left alone in his playpen or his crib may become completely engrossed in playing and messing about with his feces. For every child his own products are of great importance. Urination and defecation now occur more in response to the specific stimuli of a full bladder and rectum, and holding back is as pleasurable as letting go. The mouth still remains important as the organ for experiencing pleasure, and will, for that matter, remain so throughout life, but the greatest intensity is displaced. Now that the child can sit and walk independently and understands the spoken word, the time has come for toilet training.

The development of motor coordination proceeds spontaneously; the development of cleanliness is brought about, just like that of speech, only in interaction with the mother. Therefore the time has now come to discuss this interaction once more, this time from the point of view of the development of emotional bonds.

# 4 THE DEVELOPMENT OF EMOTIONAL BONDS WITH THE ENVIRONMENT

The infant's earliest emotions are probably very diffuse and largely unconscious. They are directed less toward the mother herself than to her breast—or toward the bottle-giving figure.

The first feelings toward the mother are very closely bound up with the satisfaction of the baby's needs. He has a vague internal image of her, which is directly connected with feeding and care. When the mother is not engaged in this, there is no inner mother image. We have seen that about the eighth month the baby is fully capable of distinguishing his mother from others. But he is not yet able to sustain his feelings for his mother when she is not present.

From direct gratification arises the bond with the mother herself, but not until the end of the early infantile period—often well into the third year—can the child maintain a stable internal bond with his parents by himself. By then there are quite enough memory traces, but his internal equilibrium required a great many experiences of security and tenderness.

We have said that the parents represent reality for him. This means that they are the objects not only of all his affection but of all his anger. If a lamp falls over because he has pulled himself upright by it, then for his limited understanding of causality it is his mother's fault. If his father cannot repair the broken balloon, that is a catastrophe which turns his father into an arbitrary tyrant, who sometimes does and sometimes does not do what the child wants. His simultaneous feelings of intense affection and intense rage—helpless rage—make it hard for the child to keep up a positive expectation when his father or mother vanishes from his horizon. Infants are dependent on their parents for the actual maintenance of life. This makes both affection and helpless rage, love and hate, so much stronger than they will be in any later phase of life, at any rate in a normal development. For the fifteen-month-old, feeling love and hate toward the same person with such intensity does not yet pose a problem. His personality is not yet well enough developed to have inner conflicts about such things. His fears are directed toward the outside world, the strange world of giants who at one time set everything right and at another are responsible for a stomach-ache or the very unpleasant sensations that accompany an attack of grippe. In their arbitrary omnipotence they suddenly take away your latest discovery, father's hammer, which you were just so splendidly waving about; they interrupt your most absorbing occupations in order to set you down at the table in front of foods that are out of your reach, except for the zwieback that appears on your plate—when? ever? after waiting half an eternity?

Every absence of these large autocrats can be experienced as desertion. All is still well, at least for a short time, if it is only one of the two who is absent. Usually, however, not only the departure but the return leads to furious protest, which is still stronger if both have been away. The poor sitter is taken aback when the little one, who so sweetly enjoyed her exclusive attention, starts to scream as soon as the parents return. It is just this vehement helpless rage that makes it so hard for the child to endure absence; and when this is not sufficiently taken into consideration, a disorganization of the developmental process may arise.

Incidentally, I wish to make it clear that I find that a young mother has the right, and must be enabled, to look after her small child herself. The danger that the child runs if he is looked after by paid guardians too early and for too great a part of the day is easily underestimated. The basis of emotional health, of psychic strength, is undermined by exposing the child too soon and too long to these violent feelings of rage and abandonment. Mothers and young children should therefore be considered for assistance when there is no breadwinner. Being cared for by his own mother has great advantages for the child over being cared for in a day nursery.

The child who has in his early years developed an adequate feeling of security toward his mother achieves independence more easily and can better endure her absence at work. As in the case of many developmental processes, it is a question of finding the right moment. The young woman who has with pleasure expended a great deal of time and care on her baby and young child thereby lays the foundation of her own freedom to go back to work away from home. If she starts this too soon, she runs the risk that the physical and psychic well-being of her child will suffer to such an extent that her freedom will be still more limited. Only in cases where the normal mother-child bond does not come into existence, where the mother is unable to give the child enough security in some other way, can a day nursery or a medical day-care center provide a solution. It is then sometimes possible to help the mother through a difficult period and to restore the mother-child relationship.

27

These are, nevertheless, paradoxes that occur frequently in bringing up children. Parents who want no trouble from their children generally have troublesome children; parents who think that their toddler should keep off all the furniture have children that sit on everything; parents who try to start toilet training at birth run a greater risk of having a child with enuresis—and so on. Only the right intensity of the demand and the right moment for it offers a chance of success. If a pedagogical demand is made too soon, too strongly, or too inconsistently, the result may be interactions between parents and child that bring about exactly the situation that was to be avoided.

# 5   TOILET TRAINING

The doctor more often becomes concerned over toilet training than over any other part of a child's upbringing. It is a culturally determined process that is carried out differently in different cultures. In our culture the most reasonable form appears to be this: When the child can sit and walk independently and begins to attach importance to his excretions and there begins to appear, moreover, a certain degree of regularity in these, the moment has come to accustom the child, in play, to the potty. If no conflict arises between parent and child, all may go quickly and easily; some children have greater difficulty; in these cases one should wait a few weeks and start over again.

Toilet training is accomplished by means of the bond with the mother. Only for his mother's sake is the child prepared to deposit his feces or his urine in the intended place. Anything that disturbs the bond with the mother also disturbs the process of toilet training, and if the mother shows impatience or becomes very angry with the child, that in itself makes it still more difficult.

Some mothers need a great deal of support in this process, and doctors often make grave mistakes either by encouraging too great strictness or by not realizing that a complaint in another field is connected with a poorly conducted toilet-training program. I am thinking particularly of disturbances in sleeping and eating.

Difficulties in falling asleep occur in this period as a result of (a) the child's difficulty in giving up his active running about at a given moment in order to go to sleep; (b) his fear of being separated from his mother; (c) too rapid toilet training, which makes the child afraid to go to sleep for fear of wetting his bed. The doctor must be fully informed of this, and whenever sleeping disturbances occur in a child between one and two years old he must inquire whether the mother is engaged in toilet training, and if so, how she is going about it. If the child's enthusiasm over the newly discovered possibility of saying "no" causes a clash of wills over toilet training, the whole process is made enormously more difficult and the child develops great anxiety.

If the training proceeds satisfactorily, the child will oblige his mother if he feels like it, if he is well disposed toward her, and he will not oblige her if he is angry with her. The products of his body, the feces and the urine, have become material for negotiation. The mother is expected to appreciate them as gifts if they are deposited in the proper manner. In this naive way the ground may be prepared for a real pleasure in giving, in generosity. However, the child can also hold back his "gifts" for a time, in resistance to his mother.

It is a fundamental mistake to attack this constipation with an intensive physical examination or with medications or enemas. Such overpowerings may break the growing will. They may also perhaps increase stubbornness. In no case do they have a favorable effect on the toilet-training process or on character development. If the child develops constipation, it is much better to suspend the training demands for a little while and treat the constipation by means of diet.

Let me remark in passing that such constipation is found particularly if the mother is pregnant at the time. In this case it is particularly important that the doctor not only have a clear understanding of the physical situation, but can form a true picture of the entire family situation and above all of the relationship between mother and child. Simple good advice can then prevent great harm in the child's development.

In normal development bowel control usually precedes bladder control. Up to the fifth year one should really not speak of nocturnal enuresis, for it is simply a matter of fast or slow maturation. The child looks upon his urine and feces as valuable possessions and is proud of his body products and happy to have them admired by his mother. When his mother's admiration stops and the urine and feces disappear into the toilet as something "dirty," he feels hurt and misunderstood. This pride in his body products is part of his awakening self-esteem. Its intensity is often not grasped by the parents, and the child does not understand why they no longer consider these body products beautiful. The exclamations over the fine heap in the potty now become, "it's dirty and goes down the toilet." The child then feels that he is loved only for his good behavior and not for his own personality as he understands it.

The difficulties that usually accompany toilet training must certainly not make us forget that becoming trained is a major cultural achievement for the child, of which he is rightly proud and in which he takes as great satisfaction as in all other accomplishments. Therefore lack of this training is just as unfavorable for the child's development as the much more frequent excessively early intensive training.

# 6 THE CHILD OF
TWO AND A HALF
TO FIVE YEARS

The child of two and a half is usually definitely finished with the creeping stage: he talks, runs through the house, in a quiet neighborhood he may run around the block by himself, and in any case he plays by himself in the yard or on the porch, although he still needs —certainly in the first half of his third year—a great deal of contact with his mother. He is starting to scrawl with a pencil, he understands a great many things well and a great many things not at all; he knows perfectly well that Daddy is coming home and says happily, "Daddy's gone to work"—but work means nothing more than going away and coming back.

When the two-year-old has a birthday party, a birthday often means nothing as yet; gifts overwhelm him, and he is unable to join in games with others for more than a few moments. The three-year-old greets his guests, will certainly get into a fight in the course of two hours, but will take pleasure in receiving gifts, though probably it will still be altogether too much for him.

What has happened in that year? Children have changed from little creatures that merely got in their mother's way to playmates, even though the comradeship is not yet of very long duration. If the children see each other often and the mothers also get together, a playmate soon becomes part of the family.

The concept "Auntie Mia's Petey" has become clear to the three-year-old, which it was not to the two-year-old.

He also knows that Auntie Mia is Petey's mommy and that Petey sleeps in her house.

Reality has become greatly expanded, and the relations between people are beginning to play a role in it. With the expansion of reality the child also feels himself more directly confronted with the fact of his own smallness in comparison with adults.

The three-year-old learns better and better to distinguish himself from the adults. He confuses himself less with his father and mother, though they still remain quite remarkable beings, far above ordinary humanity. An authoritarian upbringing reinforces this overvaluation and undermines the sense of reality in that respect. From the moment that the child makes a distinction between himself and his mother and father, it becomes the parents' task to help him discover the limitations of their personalities. If the child can also rely on his observations concerning his parents, he will develop more vigorously; but one must not outstrip his development and his strength. The discovery that you yourself as a small child are really separate from those powerful beings, your parents, is a painful one, and it is then particularly necessary to be able to fortify your own helplessness with their strength.

As almost everywhere in child rearing, it is well to leave the initiative to the child, but one must also recognize where differences exist. "Ha, mommy spilled," says the four-year-old with pride, for he himself can carry a full glass a little way; but in a thunderstorm, which still frightens him, it is not yet good for him to see that his mother is also frightened. Children can stand a great deal as long as they have their parents nearby (Freud & Burlingham, 1943).

From a preventive point of view this is important. It means that it is better for the mother to go into the doctor's consulting room with the child rather than stay in the waiting room, even though he may possibly cry more. It means that frequent visits by the mother when the child is in the hospital and partial care by her is better than forbidding visits to avoid crying at her departure (Bergmann & Freud, 1955). It also means that while playing, the child must for a long time yet be able to turn to his mother whenever he wants to. When he plays outdoors, he likes to have the door left ajar.

The three-year-old is happy to play independently, but he wants to be able to bring his mother into his play at any moment. Now, it is naturally not a very serious matter if he discovers that this is not always possible. He can then notice that he becomes angry at this and discover that this anger does not destroy the bond between them. Sometimes the mother becomes annoyed at what she considers his pestering, and he notices that, although she gets angry, she also gets over her anger.

The child's adjustment to reality is brought about through a constant trying out and testing. There is also a constant imitation of adults, which turns into fantasy play about the third year. The two-year-old takes a rag and rubs and polishes with it just like his mother; the three-year-old still does that too, but he also turns a chair upside-down and rides around the room in his "car," honking loudly. On his upside-down chair he is Daddy going to work. He fishes the discarded mail out of the wastebasket, hangs a handbag over his shoulder, and is the mailman. Today I'm the pussycat," says the little girl between meows as she crawls around the room.

This fantasy play offers the possibility of dealing with difficult feelings through play. The little girl who punishes her dolls by putting them to bed, the little boy who spanks his teddy bear because it has wet the bed, are translating a difficult situation into an active form. The little girl has not been put to bed, but she puts the doll to bed; the little boy, who may never have been spanked for being wet, portrays his conflict over toilet training by means of the teddy bear.

During this period we can make effective use of fantasy play in exceptionally difficult situations. In the children's wards of hospitals a constantly increasing number of play therapists help children depict in play the excessively burdensome situation of the hospital stay with all its attendant horrors. This simple measure makes it easier to deal with a crisis of this sort. Parents will often need to be persuaded to permit similar play at home after a situation that has been painful for the child. The child who has been to the dentist plays dentist the next day and tries to force open the doll's mouth—or, if he has the chance, his little brother's or sister's. Again it is the active repetition of what has been passively experienced, which we have already seen in the case of throwing the blocks out of the playpen. But now the active repetition has acquired the nature of play even for the child himself. Sometimes the play takes on a quite serious character, as in dealing with an illness or a separation.

The mother of a three-year-old girl had for the first time been absent for a few days. When she returned, she brought the child a doll. The child immediately named the doll "Mommy" and threw it down the stairs, brought it back, and threw it down again. In this way she communicated to her mother how angry and sad she had been about the separation. And with that her anger was over.

This fantasy play takes on such intensity only between the third and the sixth year. We may also call it role playing; it is a way of becoming familiar with things, in which the sense of reality can be set aside and picked up again and remains partly outside of the play.

"Look out, you'll fall in the water!" screams a boy in horror as his mother steps off the rug onto the bare floor, which for him is for the moment the open sea.

"I'm a big man, and you've got to call me Mister," says he, but the big man makes no protest at being picked up and set down at the table. It is a great pity that adults can no longer do this. It has great charm.

"Are you a cop or a robber?" asks the five-year-old of his three-year-old brother. "I'm just kind of a plain man," answers the little one, taken aback.

"Later I'll be big," announces the little girl at the table, "and then you'll be little, and then I'll marry Daddy and you'll be our baby."

"When is Daddy going to die?" asks the little boy. "Then I'll marry you."

From such fantasy play it is evident how much more personal the child's relation to his parents and to reality has become. Little brothers and sisters are no longer objects to be thrown away, but personalities in their own right with whom you have to reckon in a particular way.

Up to now we have looked upon the small child as a solitary individual with a mother and a father, and possibly a cat. From now on we can no longer do this. Now it makes a distinct difference whether the child is the oldest or has to take a stand amid the older ones. A child who gets a little brother or sister lets his feeling toward the baby be determined in part by that of his parents. When his mother tells him about the dear little baby that is coming, the child knows that a baby is something to be found lovable, and he too finds it lovable—and, moreover, like anything new, pleasantly exciting. Whether or not he has been properly prepared, the three- to five-year-old will have his own thoughts about the pregnancy and may possibly show them in his play. Thus I once saw a little girl quite seriously fit her teddy bear onto her father's abdomen and suddenly make it jump up. Obviously her mother's explanation that babies grow inside their mothers had made an impression, but still had led to play about birth through the abdominal wall, in which it made no difference whether this took place in the father or in the mother.

Besides curiosity, interest, and tenderness, all children of this age also feel jealousy because the mother devotes so much attention to the baby. Two-year-olds express this openly: they run to the crib and hit the baby if one of the parents does not intervene. In somewhat older children expressions of jealously are held in leash.

Jealousy between children often reappears when the youngest has begun to walk and is steady enough on his feet to defend himself and his possessions. Then the second half of the third year is characterized by attack and screaming and counterattack until the children really begin to play together a bit. Even then an important part is still played by the marking out of territories, defense of possessions, competition for the attention of the mother or the father.

It is strange that we who live in a competitive society are inclined either to minimize or to deny the open and vehement rivalry between children. It is as if we still cherished something of the illusion of the purity of a child's soul. In the routine treatment of a pregnancy the doctor should include preparing the mother for this jealousy and finding out how the children and the family are prepared for the arrival of another baby.

The child's normal belligerence is stifled by many parents, while at the same time they are anxious to have enterprising children who can hold their own on the street and in class. Perhaps this is due to the fact that, though the belligerence of a young child with his limited strength is not dangerous, it takes quite violent forms. He hits, kicks, stamps, and is not yet restrained by the rules of sportsmanship or good manners. Only slowly does he learn that his brother will exact revenge for a kick and that his mother disapproves of it. Only very slowly do comradeship and affection restrain his pugnacity.

The sense of reality develops with experience. The child naturally learns quickly that he himself feels pain when he is punched. When he himself punches, he feels pleasure; and from this to the realization that what gives him pleasure gives someone else pain is a big step. The next step is that it is pleasurable to cause pain, but that this leads to retaliation. The step following this brings the ability to sympathize with another's pain and thus perhaps to stop causing pain.

In the preceding phase, interest in one's excretions stood in the foreground. During the second year the child discovers his own genitals, and at two to two and a half years sex differences as well, and the genitals then start to become the center of interest. There now develops a complicated constellation of instinctual drives and emotions, also influenced by the progressive development of the whole personality, which we summarize as the *oedipal situation.*

Perhaps this is the proper place to point out once more that no single phase of development has a clearly defined course. Each following phase begins without the preceding one having ended, and traces of earlier phases always remain in existence; moreover, the rate of development differs greatly in different children. The ages of which I speak are therefore only roughly approximate and serve merely as focal points.

When I say that the child discovers the distinction between the sexes in his third year, this sounds a little as if it took place from one day to the next. Sometimes, in fact, it seems to happen in this way. The little girl who has often seen her little brother diapered and bathed may suddenly draw the conclusion from repeated observation that something about him is different. But even if there is no baby of the other sex in the family, sooner or later there comes a point at which the child becomes interested in the genitals and notices that they are different in her playmates.

It makes a difference whether children make this observation on other children or on their parents. In both cases, however, it is an observation that at first does not register. Even if the child consciously sees the difference and speaks about it, it may often be denied again at a later time. This is the more striking since children of this age are particularly observant. In the period when the excretory functions are of great interest, the child discovers that his feces and urine are not an essential part of his body but can be discarded without danger. We have already seen that this often gives rise at first to some anxiety and that later the mastery of toilet training becomes an achievement. Something of the same sort occurs now. The boy as well as the girl at first interpret the female genitalia exclusively as the lack of a penis and testes, and both feel themselves threatened thereby. The little girl feels as if she were lacking something, as if something had been taken from her, or as if she had been victimized. The boy is afraid that what is lacking in the little girl could also be lost by him. If children discover the sexual differences in their parents, they feel even more threatened, since the pubic hair and the difference in size look frighteningly weird to them.

To this is added the fact that many parents find it difficult to talk openly with their young children about sex differences. Not only do the children deny their interest in the subject; their parents refuse to admit their children's interest and fail to answer their questions, which at this point are quite direct and detached. Most parents are, in fact, prepared to tell children that babies grow inside their mother; and bright children define little Peter not as Auntie Mia's little boy, but in terms of "Petey came out of Auntie Mia's belly."

They find comfort and support in this idea, but the mother runs the risk that her Charlie will suddenly start stuffing himself with food or holding back his bowel movements in order to make a baby grow in his own belly.

To three-year-olds, sex is a constant topic of conversation. What is the penis for, why do girls have a split, why don't boys have babies, why don't girls have penises, why is it that mothers have breasts and little girls don't, why is it that girls get breasts when they grow up and boys don't? Why does Daddy have a big penis and Charlie a little one? If one gives children real freedom, these are questions that are thoroughly discussed.

Why are children entitled to an opportunity to ask such questions and to get honest answers, even though we know that their emotional development alone will lead them to accept only the male genitalia as real? To the little girl, the information that boys cannot get breasts or have babies grow in their bellies is no valid excuse for her mother not giving her a penis *now*. The little boy would be glad to believe his mother when she says that his penis grew like that, is part of him, and will get larger, but he still entertains a doubt already prepared in the preceding period. After all, he also considered his feces as a part of himself, and that was something that actually disappeared. In spite of these ideas, which cannot be entirely corrected through enlightenment, I find that children's questions must be answered. For we want an honest relationship with our children and would not like them to feel that they are being given a runaround over things about which they are thinking seriously. The fact that they use their intelligence to organize their observation is inspiring, something that we are happy to encourage and do not want to stifle.

This is not, however, entirely a matter of the development of the intellect. With the discovery of the difference between the sexes the development of instinctual life also enters another phase. The libido and aggression become more personally directed. The wish to own, to take possession of the mother or the father, that played such an important role in the preceding phase, turns into a "courtship." In the beginning both the little boy and the little girl court the mother, and both want to take the father's place with her, but with the growing psychic importance of sex distinction this begins to change. The courtship becomes more personal, more aggressive, the little boy proudly shows his mother his penis; he wants to eliminate his father as a rival. Naturally the emotions are not involved all day long. On the contrary, the father whom he wants to put aside at one moment is the same father who has to help him in the next moment with something that he cannot manage, the same father into whose lap he confidently climbs. Yet it is no coincidence that in just this period children think and talk so much about dying. "Dead" and "away" are, to begin with, synonymous, and it is obvious that the boy who spends the entire day playing "grown-up" as mailman, pilot, garbage collector, also wants to be the father. "When you're a hundred years old you'll be dead, won't you?" says the four-year-old boy confidentially. "And when you're two hundred, will you still be alive?" he continues.

This is not, on the whole, a weighty matter, and parents do not take it too seriously. It is not of great significance for the bystander, but for the child it is a truly important phase, in which the emotions are not stronger but much more personal than in the preceding one. The desire to be his mother's husband really means to the little boy something like being in love; the sexual tension that arises is discharged in infantile masturbation. Parents often threaten their children about this: "The doctor will have to cut it," "You'll get sick," "That's very unhealthy," "That's dirty and babyish." But in my experience they seek help only when the situation has become really serious. The doctor must therefore not meet complaints about infantile masturbation with a simple reassurance, but must find out exactly what the child does, when he does it, and what his facial expression is while he does it. This will often bring to the parents' attention the fact that the child looks anxious at the time. In this case the masturbation does not represent release of tension, but rather a constant need to reassure himself that his penis is still there—an indication of increased anxiety. If the complaint comes from the school rather than from the parents, this may indicate an unfavorable situation within the family.

But let us return to the matter of normal development.

Even in normal development, anxieties occur in this phase. The little boy who, while he was being dressed in the morning, showed his mother proudly how nicely he could urinate may suddenly show anxiety in his bath, or develop an aversion to washing. The background of such anxiety does not always become manifest. Symptoms of this sort are of a transient nature and do not by any means always require treatment. Parents will often take no notice of them and will merely say, "Don't be so silly." But the small boy, who in the preceding phase had great difficulty in learning that it is usual for his feces to disappear, now has a tendency to transfer his original anxiety about his feces to the genitals from which he now derives such great pleasure. He believes that these too may sometime come off in the bath or disappear, the more so since he interprets the girl's genitals as a lost penis.

This is a period in which surgical procedures are especially poorly tolerated. For instance, a tonsillectomy, which is sometimes necessary because of recurrent ear infections, may be interpreted as, "They're really going to cut into me, the doctor can really cut something away all of a sudden." But even without such procedures the child who was so dauntless over falls and bumps during the period of learning to walk may now suddenly become a crybaby and carry on over a small cut of his finger as if this were a real castration.

This entire constellation is subsumed in the *positive Oedipus complex.*

At some particular moment in his development, the child discovers the futility of his wishes toward his mother. She snaps at him, or bundles him off to bed when he has been naughty, belittles him, laughs at him; and if, in addition to all this, he finds his genitals merely an anxiety-producing possession, which may go exactly the same way as the girl's, he anticipates his fears and decides he would rather be a girl. This is a desire that a boy in our culture dare not express—which makes it no easier for him to overcome his anxiety. This desire to be a girl and his father's wife, which is thus linked with a turning toward the father, we call the *negative Oedipus complex.* A boy's desire to be a girl not only conflicts with the cultural pattern but is also an anxiety-producing wish, for it presupposes in the world of his imagination the loss of that organ of which he is at the same time so proud.

Under the pressure of the anxieties of this period, the positive and negative Oedipus complexes may alternate for a time. Along with this, the child's development continues. His insight into reality broadens out; his usual affection for his parents exists alongside all these confusing emotions and, in fact, develops through them to a much more personal way of feeling affection for another, which is important for his later love life.

Before we describe how this phase comes to an end, let us return to the development of the girl. We have seen how she too at first competes actively for her mother and wants to replace her father, just as the boy does. But at the same time she believes that her mother is responsible for what she thinks of as the removal of the important organ. Anger, which already exists as a result of all the pedagogical conflicts, over toilet training among others, is now greatly strengthened. This inaugurates the turning toward the father.

For the mother this can be a troublesome period, since the little girl in this phase is so difficult to manage, and yet she must cope with her all day long. Development proceeds most harmoniously if the child looks upon her parents as a unit and cannot play one off against the other. For the girl as well as the boy, there is for a time an alternation between, on the one hand, the negative Oedipus complex (in this case, wanting to take her father's place with her mother—which in her development thus precedes the positive (wanting to take her mother's place with her father)—and, on the other hand, the turning toward the father and wanting to get a baby from him, like her mother. (This manifests itself to an increased extent if the mother gives birth during this time.) The disappointment over the impossibility of this then forces the child back into active competition for the mother, and these two adjustments continue to interweave for a time (Lampl-de Groot, 1927).

It is just in this period that the growth of the sense of reality forms an important facet of character development. Questions such as "What is this?" and "What is that?" are continually asked in the second half of the third year.

To be "deceived" in fundamental things in answer to these questions is a serious hindrance to the entire development. For the child himself needs considerable courage to realize that there is much that he does not understand. Although one is constantly impressed by what children of two and a half can understand, they themselves are quite angry over what they do not yet understand.

Observation and experience make up a large part of the small child's task and it is no wonder that he seeks consolation for his failure to understand so many things by falling back on his rich experience. Thus five-year-old Robert says, "Do you believe that there's a God?" and follows thus up consolingly with "Well, I don't think it's likely."

Finding analogies now plays an important role in thinking. The vocabulary increases rapidly. The word "I" begins to play a role in the three-year-old's speech. The thought processes usually run ahead of the ability to articulate, so that at the beginning of the third year stammering and hesitation in speaking are common, without having any real pathological significance.

Speech begins to arrange itself grammatically. Betty, two years and three months old, on arriving home from vacation says with a sigh of relief, "Nice bed, sleep nice." Ann, five years old, in making plans for the next day will name the correct times and the correct order of events, though in doing so she will not always subordinate her wishes to considerations of reality.

And now the time has come to repair an omission and to describe as a whole the influence of language on the child's development.

# 7 THE DEVELOPMENT OF SPEECH

We have seen the first smile and the first following of movement with the eyes as the earliest evidence that mother-child contact has become adequately established. Quite soon the infant begins to have greater need of social contact; he expresses this, as he expresses everything, by crying, and he is delighted when his father or his mother picks him up. It is then no longer a question of hunger alone, but of sociability.

At the age of about three months the baby in his crib can be heard amusing himself by making sounds. This vocalizing constantly increases in the following months and acts as preliminary practice for speaking. Mothers react to it as if they knew this, for they prattle in answer—and the baby finds that enchanting.

The first words are spoken about the end of the first year. The first "ma-ma" or "da-da" is certainly a true communication, but does not yet represent the use of the word as a symbol. The first words are called need-words. "Ma-ma," "da-da" may just as well signify "I have a stomach ache" as "I need companionship," "I have a wet diaper," "I'm hungry," or "That's a pretty sound." The "ma-ma," "da-da" still arises directly out of the practice for speech in prattling, in which the baby produces such magnificently rolled r's, such splendid *kr-kr* sounds, and finally practices the other consonants as well, in the course of which practice "ma-ma" and "da-da" occur very soon.

The discovery of the symbolic significance of the

word, the actual function of naming, is quite as great a discovery as that of walking. But while walking will always take place if it is not prevented, talking will evolve only in interaction with the environment. Let me quote an account of an experiment made in the reign of the Holy Roman Emperor Frederick II, in the thirteenth century (Salimbene, n.d.).

> ...He wanted to find out what kind of speech and what manner of speech children would have when they grew up, if they spoke to no one beforehand. So he bade foster mothers and nurses to suckle the children, to bathe and wash them, but in no way to prattle with them or speak to them, for he wanted to learn whether they would speak the Hebrew language, which was the oldest, or Greek, or Latin, or Arabic, or perhaps the language of their parents, of whom they had been born. But he labored in vain, because the children all died. For they could not live without the petting and the joyful faces and loving words of their foster mothers. And so the songs are called "swaddling songs," which a woman sings while she is rocking the cradle, to put a child to sleep, and without them a child sleeps badly and has no rest.

This truth still holds. The modern version is to be found in Spitz's (1965) *The First Year of Life*. Children with whom no one talks, with whom there is no social contact, for whom there is no mother-child relationship, have a very poor chance of life, unless a foster mother takes on the task of the mother in this respect. But in normal development the child can discover the naming of objects in his second year, and then pointing and giving names to things becomes one of his most engaging occupations. In this he is not always prepared to conform to the rules of grown-up language, but often gives things names of his own coining. In the course of normal learning this practice dies out on its own. The ability to form analogies and thus to find new names is one of the most important precursors of what we shall describe as secondary-process thinking.

The first sentences are one-word sentences: "cook-cook," or "too-too," means "I want a cookie." It is most remarkable that the child who can pronounce the consonants so well in his prattling finds them so much more difficult when he uses the word as a symbol; "cook-cook" is just as easy to say as "too-too." And although the child in jabbering has quite often said "aw-aw" or "oh-oh," "auto" very easily becomes "toe-toe" or something similar (Meijers, 1962). However, if the mother does not join in the baby talk, but herself pronounces the words correctly, this will soon correct itself; and at the end of the second year the child knows a fairly large number of words.

The first words are nouns. Only slowly are two-word sentences formed, either with adjectives or with verbs: "Mommy—nice," "Dolly—seep [sleep]" and so on. Gradually sentence structure develops, and this development indicates not only the development of proper word usage, but equally the potentiality for logical thought.

In this connection it is certainly no coincidence that places are named much earlier than times, and that incorrect use of time indications continues for quite a while: "When I had a birthday tomorrow," and so on. For that matter, an adult need only try to plan an organized argument to discover that thinking is hard work. Speech does not require as careful attention to grammatical structure as the written word. We can prove this with almost any speaker if we listen, not to the sense, but to the form of his discourse. Spontaneous thought is not so strictly logical as we in our adult arrogance believe. It consists of fragments of sentences, interspersed with figures of speech that have no particularly strong logical connection, but more often an associative or even a sound-associative connection. Nevertheless, it all has a dynamic coherence, not only with the sense of the subject about which we happen to be thinking, but also with all that concerns us emotionally.

This brings me to the next point. Speech disturbances do not by any means always have to do with a delay in the maturation of speech as such, or of logical thinking as such, but very often with emotional problems. We are all familiar with the stammering of the two-and-a-half- to three-year-old, which is not based so much on poor speech development as on a superabundance of subject matter, but which is also frequently connected with toilet-training problems. With children in whom a definite stutter develops, one can sometimes prevent a fixation of the habit by letting them say the dirty words they are suppressing too vigorously.

This stuttering, then, is really built up as a neurotic symptom: a specific impulse is suppressed—in this case the impulse to say dirty words. Unconsciously a compromise is reached, whereby both tendencies continue: the child speaks poorly, but the forbidden words do not come to the surface. Sometimes saying the dirty words is enough; children go in for this with great enthusiasm and then after a little while leave off quite normally.

Sometimes it is really a question of toilet-training problems, and thus not of dirty words as such. Then it is desirable to drop the demands of toilet training temporarily. In these cases the stuttering expresses a neurotic compromise in a physical symptom. We have already described this as conversion. Since such cases of stuttering do not arise out of a conflict in the preceding period, Fenichel (1945) speaks of a pregenital conversion neurosis.

I have also repeatedly seen stuttering and stammering in small children in connection with the conflicts of the oedipal phase. In these cases the origin often lay in a direct rivalry with the more fluent speech of an older sister, who was expressing her own conflicts over being a girl by means of a torrent of words.

In many cases of speech disturbances in adults we have to return to the period of toilet training in order to find the cause. People who feel hampered in expressing their thoughts, especially in putting their feelings into words, or who, on the other hand, tend toward verbosity and diffuseness, may thereby indicate a connection with earlier games in urination. Sometimes this has served to put me on the track of an enuresis that the patient himself had forgotten, although he had suffered severely from it as a child.

Comprehension of the spoken word occurs long before speech itself. About the end of the first year children already understand much more than they can put into words. In the second year this may be observed even more convincingly. The understanding of connections expresses itself, for example, in the desire to carry out actions to the full. If the blocks are to be put in the box, they must all be put in; if things are thrown away, they are all thrown away with great pleasure—and so on. There is a tendency toward logical completion of the job, and from this we may conclude that a thought process takes place in the child's mind.

The same holds true of the ability to follow simple commands. The mother may say, for example, "Here, help me with your stocking" or, "Now pull up your pants," and the child understands, even though he is not yet able to talk.

The great pleasure that the child takes in walking in the first half of the second year is equaled in the second half by his pleasure in naming of things. Logical thinking no longer gives elementary "functional pleasure" (*Functionslust*). For some time yet a child may be heard carefully trying out new discoveries; he then looks stealthily toward the grown-ups to see whether they agree, whether the word was used correctly, whether the sentence was well constructed. It is unfortunate for the child if every discovery is applauded or every mistake is laughed at. The child's errors in speaking are no doubt often captivating to the adults, but the child derives more benefit from necessary correction. Even affectionate laughter over what is to him perfectly serious gives the child the impression that he is being ridiculed, and this may have a very detrimental influence on his self-respect.

The child still has few concepts at his command and must thus take over a great deal from the adults without quite understanding. If one asks a child of two and a half, "Where's Daddy?" and he says, "Daddy's gone to work"—or rather, "Daddy—work"—that is for the child no more than what Mommy or Daddy has always said about it, with the connotation of, "He goes away at a particular time of day and comes back again at a given time." Here we see one of the most important functions of speech: it is a magic formula that helps the child to bridge the distance between Daddy's going away and Daddy's coming back. "Daddy—work" means, "Daddy still exists even when he's not home"—a very difficult step for the child.

The development of speech is also an important phase in the achievement of independence. This is easily seen in children who already think a great deal but cannot speak yet; they often have a period before the breakthrough of speech in which they are difficult and intractable. We see this much more clearly, naturally, in children who never achieve speech—that is, in pathological cases, into which I cannot go here.

Naming confers power, and thinking in words, considering, working things through by thinking, are perhaps the most important ways in which man can deal with his environment and especially with his own impulses. Thus one may sometimes see in children who have learned to talk and have developed good sentence structure a drastic change in character. They have changed from babies into little people. The use of "I" about the third year indicates that the child has really come to distinguish himself from his mother, that he has really become an independent personality. Very soon he will be able to answer such questions as, "Who are you?" "What's your name?" and "How old are you?"—all questions that attempt to describe the identity. "Who are you?" will, unless the mother has given rigorous practice, be answered only with the given name, and the age may be told by holding up three fingers. This holding up of the fingers is more in the nature of a stunt than a true insight into the meaning of the number, but it still means to the child something like "I am so-and-so, I am thus-and-thus, I am a girl, I am a boy, I am Betty, I am three years old."

Some children continue for a long time to use the given name to refer to themselves: "Bobby says," and so on. Often that points to incomplete individuation, or at least to individuation which still needs to evolve further toward the "I." Like all processes, the development of individuation runs its course at a different tempo in different children.

It is a great step from "Mommy do" to "Mommy, will you do this or that?" and from "Petey, ow!" to "Mommy, I bumped my knee!" This last example is not a very good one, for the likelihood is that Peter, at the moment when he bumps his knee, will not say, "Mommy, I bumped my knee," but will still cry out, "Ow, ow!" and "Mommy, Mommy!" Under the influence of emotion, speech quickly becomes less organized. This may sometimes be observed even in adults, but in children it is certainly true.

It often happens, too, that a child will return to baby talk when a younger brother or sister has reached the babbling phase. The child wants the same love that his mother gives his little brother or sister; he wants to *be* the little brother or sister to avoid having to be jealous. This leads to false baby talk, which often irritates parents. Just those parents who will not admit their children are jealous, although jealousy at the birth of a new baby is inevitable, are inclined not to recognize false baby talk consciously as an expression of jealousy, but to treat it as if it were something as reprehensible as jealousy.

There is nothing so often awakened and at the same time so little tolerated as shamming insincerity in a child.

A child who is not permitted to be jealous must do something with his jealousy and thus takes refuge in identification with the baby, in becoming like the baby, and in talking like the baby. But what the parents find charming in the baby, they see in the three- or four-year-old only as an annoying affectation. "You can say it perfectly well," they rebuke him, becoming angry.

# 8  CHILDHOOD ANXIETIES AND THEIR ASSOCIATION WITH OPERATIONS

In the oedipal phase, the child's emotions may be particularly strong and may become manifest in unexpected areas. The disturbances of the small child are symptom-poor, for the child has only a few symptoms at his disposal for expressing inner conflicts. We have already seen how anxiety can suddenly manifest itself in the bath, and anxiety is often a sign of an inner conflict, which, however, may not yet be interfering with development.

It is more difficult to form a judgment when there are also disturbances of function that are not yet indications of a lasting pathological state. A child who is preoccupied with pregnancy fantasies may have abdominal pain; but the pain need not, at this point, be interpreted as an actual expression of incipient hysteria. A child may sleep poorly because, tormented by curiosity, he feels a compulsion to investigate the parents' bedroom. This curiosity will express itself as anxiety, since the child's fantasies about what the father and the mother experience together are generally colored by anxiety.

Parents sometimes prohibit the expression of sexual curiosity on the part of the child, and this causes anxiety. Sometimes this anxiety is connected with the developmental phase in which the child pictures the sexual act as an overpowering. A child who witnesses the mating of two dogs or hears cats yowling, a country child who sees the bull mounting the cow, perceives the aggressive rather than the erotic aspect of the proceedings. Moreover, the child himself has love-hate feelings for his parents. This, added to his anger over the secrecy of the parental experiences, leads the child to interpret the sexual act as an act of aggression.

Sensible parents find a mean between yielding excessively and deserting the child in his anxiety. But parents themselves, not realizing that it is part of normal development, are often made anxious by the anxiety of their children. They see it, as it were, projected into the future and believe that the child will grow up anxiety-ridden. Especially parents who themselves suffer or have suffered from neurotic anxiety tend to induce it in their children by taking the children's anxieties too seriously and by their inability to maintain the necessary calm. An angry and reproachful attitude increases the anxiety, and the only effect is that the child will no longer dare bring it into the open. A great deal of quite genuine neurotic anxiety in children is borne in silence because they dare not confess their fears.

Normal anxiety is often intensified by painful illnesses or other traumatic events. Repeated attacks of quinsy and ear infections involving puncture of the eardrum cause the child a great deal of pain, for which, of course, he holds the adults responsbile. He fears his parents as well as the doctor, who is part of the world of the loved-hated parents. Good preventive care and proper mental hygiene help to provide as good a climate as possible in which the surgical intervention can take place. This means, first of all, that the child should not be deceived. It should be made clear to the parents that they must explain things honestly. The doctor himself should reveal in detail what is going to happen, taking into account the child's condition. A deaf child can make nothing of the best verbal explanation, and at the height of a middle-ear infection a child will perhaps derive more benefit from a demonstration on a doll than from an explanation that he can scarcely hear and that is impeded by the earache. But in any case, the child must know in advance that the intervention will take place and how it will take place.

Pain forms a threat to the child's whole personality. He will react to it afterward as if his parents had inflicted it on him intentionally, and the most careful explanation may be taken as hypocritical cajolery.

I shall give two examples of this. Julie said to her mother a few months after her tonsillectomy, "Mommy, those breasts of yours—they can come off now that little brother is weaned. You just get a little prick, and then you go to sleep and you don't know anything about it." That was literally the explanation that had been given to her before the tonsillectomy. "After all," said she, "they're not good for anything any more"—exactly what her father had said about her tonsils. To a little girl a tonsillectomy is quite as serious a matter as a breast amputation is to a grown woman; one must not underestimate the anxieties aroused by these "innocent" interventions.

The psychiatrist is not accustomed to having his treatment meet with immediate success. On the contrary, he more often gives lengthy treatment and must be content with moderate success. But when he sees children quite soon after the surgical procedure by which they have been psychically traumatized, he can occasionally witness a dramatic recovery. I once saw such a recovery in a small child whose intellectual development had greatly retrogressed after a tonsillectomy. He acted in every way like a retarded child, and the parents were highly disturbed when they came to me. In the first hour this boy drew a picture of the doctor's car going up in flames. In the second hour he had the doctor, car and all, drive into the water and drown. After the third hour the parents came to tell me proudly that he was cured. His "revenge" on the doctor had been enough to set his development in motion again and to guide his feelings of hostility, through play, into acceptable channels.

Both examples are particularly illustrative for our purpose. Little Julie tries to master the traumatic experience by imagining herself doing her mother a serious injury, since she considers her mother responsible for the infliction of pain. To a small child the mother is responsible for whatever happens to the child's body, and thus also for such painful episodes.

The little boy, on the other hand, had given up maturing because he believed that maturing involved severe penalties such as the tonsillectomy. He remained in the safety of babyhood. In both cases, however, the fantasy of revenge was enough to set development going again—in the case of the girl, visualizing the amputation of the mother's breasts; in that of the boy, revenge on the doctor by means of the drawings.

Both children had very intelligent parents who were prepared to accept the revengefulness. This does not, of course, happen very often. In general, parents, taken aback, will repudiate such attempts to master the situation; yet such attempts constitute our most important tool for the prevention of later disturbances.

More and more the play therapist is becoming a part

of the pediatric clinic, helping the children to repeat actively what they have experienced passively, to act out in play all the unpleasant things that have happened to them, and to accept their anger as normal.

For an adult it is not pleasant to see a child furiously poking out the eyes of a doll after an operation for cross-eyes, piercing the arms of a teddy bear after a venipuncture, or tying up the bear after he himself has lain strapped to the operating table. But for the child this freedom to act, to depict in his role playing what he has experienced, may provide just the right opportunity for working it through, so that he may gain control of the situation and avoid neurotic reactions.

# 9  THE DECLINE OF THE OEDIPUS COMPLEX

If the preschooler develops normally, his sense of reality constantly increases. "Not true, is it?" the little boy says of the fairy tale—but his voice shows his respect for and fear of the giant. It is not only the sense of reality that is improved; more exactly, the increasingly personal quality of the emotions during the oedipal phase makes it more and more difficult for the child to tolerate the coexistence of love and rivalry. What can and what cannot be are ever more clearly distinguished with the growth of the sense of reality. "Can't be, huh, Mommy?" is said just as commonly as "I want, I want!—though there is, naturally, a long intermediate phase in which there are many questions about why it can't be.

Four main factors lead to the giving up of the oedipal wishes:

1. The growing sense of reality confronts the child with the fact that he is too little for the father or the mother, a mortification for which he consoles himself with fantasies of adulthood.

2. Increasing integration makes the alternation between love and hate harder to bear; and with a normal loving approach by the parents, love wins out.

3. Loving brings with it the fear of loss of love, and it is because of this fear that rivalry is relinquished.

4. We have already seen that both boys and girls interpret the female genitals at first as the result of the breaking off of the penis. Consequently the young child's

masturbation, which is burdened with feelings of love toward one parent and of rivalry toward the other, is constantly coupled with anxiety, even when no threats have been made.

This fear of punishment by bodily injury we have already discussed. It is one of the causes not only of the suppression of infantile masturbation, but also of the repression of the accompanying oedipal wishes and fantasies.

What becomes of all this energy now? Affection and a readiness to learn remain. The readiness to learn is, in fact, greatly increased, since in place of the boy's desire to replace the father the desire to become like the father gains the upper hand; and in the case of the girl, the desire to become like the mother. The imitation that has played such an important role in the entire oedipal period becomes a true adaptation, a modeling of oneself on the father or mother—naturally, with elements of both father and mother. With this development, the formation of the ego ideal, which up to now has tended toward the fantastic, becomes much more realistic, although there is still considerable overestimation of the father and mother. The anger against the parent with whom the child was competing becomes internalized and gives rise to the severity of the conscience.

With the disappearance of the Oedipus complex there comes into existence a group of motivations, not entirely new, but newly integrated, which we collectively call the superego. The superego, then, includes the internalized ideals as well as the internalized prohibitions of undesirable strivings.

We may carry even further the fate of the drives that

make up the Oedipus complex. The intensive sexual curiosity that played such an important role between the ages of three and a half and four and a half years has turned into a much more general thirst for knowledge. All day long the child is busy examining everything around him, and in this occupation he is sharply focused on reality. This focus must exist before there can be a real possibility of going to school and mastering the subject matter. This shift from sexual curiosity to a general eagerness to learn we call sublimation.

By sublimation is meant the possibility of using the energy of drives toward an objective entirely different from the original one. The quality of the impulse is also changed in the process, so that its origin is later unrecognizable. Only if a neurotic regression arises will this origin once more become relevant and disturbing. Sublimation emphasizes again what has already been said about the importance of answering a small child's questions about sex. Sublimation is possible only to a limited degree, differing with each person.

Man also uses many other means of coming to terms with instinctual impulses that cannot be gratified. Projection, for example, is often employed against aggressive impulses: we perceive these impulses, not in ourselves, but in others. We have already seen, too, that the anger awakened in the child by feelings of helplessness is soon transformed by identification with the parents. We have also seen how pleasure in causing pain is modified by association with others, giving rise to the potentiality for sympathy. Cleanliness develops as a reaction to the original delight in being dirty. A great many impulses, however, are repressed; they disappear from consciousness. This very repression causes the early development to disappear from the memory, so that the oedipal drives are forgotten in adulthood. It is for this reason that people who are not in frequent contact with children may be inclined to deny the existence of this early development.

The decline of the Oedipus complex leads to a structuring of the personality. Instinctual drives arouse lasting impulses and desires, which now, however, are assessed by the person himself. We describe as ego functions, then, desire for knowledge, observation, memory, the determination of which impulses may be given free rein and which may not—in short, the taking into account of outer and inner reality.

I have already described how the decline of the Oedipus complex leads to the formation of the ego ideal and of the conscience. The two together can now be distinguished from the ego and the id as the superego. The id includes all of the instinctual drives and is therefore unconscious. Only the impulses, desires, and feelings that originate in drives enter consciousness. Ego and superego are partly conscious, partly unconscious. The example of the sex differences that are at first denied illustrates how observation that is typically an ego function may be repressed and thus become unconscious. Many superego motivations are also unconscious. At puberty the boy no longer remembers how his mother threatened him when he masturbated as a small child, but explains the resultant determined rejection of onanism with "I think it's unaesthetic," or "I think it's infantile."

In a harmonious personality the structure is not noticeable. It is mainly for an understanding of disharmony that the structural grouping is important. It is useful also when we attempt to describe the great changes between the child at the height of the oedipal phase and the latency child, who is so much more ready to make demands on himself and who has partly withdrawn from the world of magic. All this sounds much more drastic than it really is. These processes take place very slowly and gradually and in a much less absolute manner than this description would indicate.

# 10   THE FIRST HALF OF
## THE LATENCY PERIOD

Latency is the period that follows the decline of the Oedipus complex and precedes the first signs of puberty. It is thus, in general, the period between the ages of five and a half and about eleven years. Naturally, we must not think of such periods as being any too precisely circumscribed.

The first half of the latency period, from about five and a half to eight years, is characterized by the remnants of the working out of the oedipal phase and by the rapid development of secondary-process thinking, which will be described in a later chapter. This type of thinking has started earlier, and its development proceeds very gradually.

We have already described how the child, even in the first year, can make a distinction between himself and the outer world. He thus gets some understanding of objective reality, primitive though it may be. This sense of reality develops further between the first and third years, and in that period he begins to get a primitive understanding of causality. The child who has several times bumped himself on the table leg avoids doing it again. In this manner even the very young child—the normal young child, at least—learns by experience.

After the decline of the Oedipus complex, secondary-process thinking develops at a quicker tempo. The child is then adjusted to reality and is interested in everything around him. The little boy knows the makes of cars better than his father and also recognizes them more quickly. In a game involving memory, the adults lose to the children. At this age children are easily taught. They can develop fantastic skill in doing jigsaw puzzles, in understanding rather complicated games—not without difficulty, and not without making mistakes, but with the growing ability to learn to abide by the rules. All children "cheat" at first, for they are anxious to win; winning in games becomes part of a victory through play in the rivalry with grown-ups. The ability to lose a game without getting angry and without feeling crushed is one of the signs that oedipal rivalry has really been conquered.

Motor skills, too, now develop quickly. This is when children learn to swim and to ride a bicycle, when they begin to take dancing lessons; they climb, learn to roller-skate, and roughhouse with father. The boy plays football on the street; the girl jumps rope. Residual castration anxiety is disposed of by means of the many pursuit games the children play. In normal children these act as a release. In the neurotic child, however, the castration anxiety is so strong and so severely repressed that in lieu of being dissipated, it is strengthened by the games. These are the very children who tend to use sadism as a defense against their anxiety. One disturbed child can make the games so terrifying as to arouse anxiety in all the others. The pursuit games may also be dangerous in the sense that they still easily overpower the sense of reality, particularly in children who need more time for resolving the Oedipus complex.

Traffic accidents frequently happen because fear of the pursuer suspends the sense of reality regarding traffic. The child's rational fear of the car that may run

67

him down has less force than the irrational fear of the child who is chasing him. Left to himself, a child of six to eight is well able to judge traffic situations and can often estimate spatial situations very well. He can also assess speeds closely enough to know whether or not he has time to cross the street. But he is still much at the mercy of his impulses, and in emotional situations his judgment does not yet have the upper hand. This is, of course, often true even of adults. Nor do children lose their heads much more easily. But in the first half of the latency period the struggle with remnants of the oedipal phase still stands in the way of rational judgment. If such emotional factors are not present, a child of six to eight can actually judge a concrete situation just as well as an adult.

Abstract logical thinking, which develops much later and much more slowly, is an entirely different matter. A rather complicated train of thought is certainly too difficult for children at this stage; often they develop a kind of pseudo logical thinking, a spurious exactitude that reminds one of the overly broad conclusions that poor statisticians draw from their data. One cold spring day I heard the following dialogue between two small boys at a pond: "Joe, let's go swimming." "Can't, it's much too cold." "Oh, no, the water's at least 70 degrees." For me that apparently exact statement of the water temperature was a particularly amusing detail. It shows how the appearance of an exact observation may be used by a child even when the content of the thought process is a simple magic wish fulfillment. If I want the water to have a summer temperature, it has; if I want this one-foot-deep pond to be deep enough for swimming, it is; and finally, if I want to be able to swim, I can.

It is this alternation between magical and logical

thinking that gives children's remarks their charm. For the sake of the adults these small children often pretend to be thinking according to the secondary process, whereas they are really, for a great part of the day, still occupied with magical notions. These grandiose fantasies betray their almost undisguised oedipal origin. Their function is clear. As the sense of reality grows, the child is more and more often confronted with failure and impotence. Self-criticism, too, increases. The child then needs comforting if he is not to become discouraged, and throughout our entire lives fantasy remains an important source of comfort in overcoming disappointments in reality. The adult may be hindered in this by the restrictions of his real life; for a child the possibilities are still much more indefinite, and he can thus more easily give his fantasies free rein.

The fantasy of being a sports champion reconciles him to the difficulties of learning to swim. The fantasy of being a concert pianist makes piano lessons more interesting—at least for most normal children. Sometimes, however, the child accepts these fantasies as reality to such an extent, and has such great difficulty in giving them up, that daydreaming discourages instead of encouraging him.

Less gifted children, but especially children with neurotic learning difficulties, may comfort themselves in school by constantly losing themselves in daydreams. Poor concentration is then added to their learning difficulties. In such cases daydreaming has a disturbing influence. For this reason educators vacillate between encouragement and discouragement of fantasying. Without fantasying, creativeness is impossible, but fantasying by no means always leads to creativeness.

It is essential to the normal function of fantasy that it be recognized as such. In neurotic development, however, there is always a remnant of magical thinking, so that wishes are treated as reality. This is true particularly of the repressed, forbidden erotic and aggressive wishes that then lead to symptom formation, since they are believed to be just as punishable as the forbidden acts. Such neurotic development may result if the child is hurt too often or too deeply. Reality becomes too painful to be accepted. The family must in this period, therefore, be a safe haven where the child is to some extent shielded. This does not, of course, apply in an absolute sense, for parents will not find everything about a six-to eight-year-old delightful and will not be sparing in their criticism. But it is a question of the form in which the criticism is expressed and whether the child senses in it at the same time an appreciation of himself as a person. Teasing and ridicule, of which parents and teachers are frequently guilty, are completely indefensible at this time. But equally harmful is the effect of overestimation, which is not an evaluation of real performance. Overestimation confuses the child in his incipient self-criticism, which may in this particular period develop into the possibility of judging one's own achievements while maintaining one's self-respect. Naturally the capacity for self-knowledge and self-criticism develops very gradually and has an entirely different appearance in a five-and-a-half-year old and in an eight-year-old. Prematurely heightened self-criticism, which one may see at times in intelligent children, indicates heightened unconscious guilt feelings and calls for further exploration.

# 11  JUDGING SCHOOL READINESS

*Readiness for kindergarten*

When is a child ready for kindergarten? In a very young healthy child there is never any lack of activity. The two-year-old is constantly busy at home. There is not always, and in city apartments practically never, enough play space. As far as that is concerned, one would be inclined to set the kindergarten age much earlier than customary. But from what we have described concerning toilet training and the separation-individuation phase it follows that several other conditions must be met before the child is able to detach himself from his mother for a few hours. The child must have reached the point where he is really conscious of being someone other than his mother, and this often does not come about until the third year.

The child learns only gradually to bridge a period of separation from his mother. Besides being able to cope with the separation, the child must also be able to maintain his toilet training independently—that is, no longer exclusively in relation to his mother but because he himself wants to. In addition, he must be able to use a toilet that is unfamiliar to him.

If still a third condition, that of inner growth, has been met, the child may go to school. This last condition includes the requirement that the child must no longer see other children exclusively as rivals in the competition for the love of the adults, but must instead be able, for a short time at least, to cooperate with them.

Going to kindergarten often starts at an unfavorable

moment, namely when a child is involved in a contest of wills with his mother or when the next baby appears and the child gets too much in the mother's way at home. Because of the strong ambivalence of the mother-child bond at such a time, the placing of the child in school has a particularly unfortunate effect.

If a child goes to kindergarten too soon, this can sometimes mark the beginning of an enduring aversion to school. It often happens that even reasonably normal children develop school phobia in such a situation, sometimes in the form of physical illness (Frijling-Schreuder, 1965b)—abdominal pain, attacks of fever, without other determinable cause. With proper treatment the prognosis is favorable, but very careful diagnosis is necessary. The proper treatment consists simply of letting the child stay home and after a few months trying again to see whether the child enjoys going to school. If, however, the symptoms are allowed to become fixed—for example, by a stubborn insistence on the child's going to school—the chances of success are meager, and a later attempt to place the child in school will result in a renewal of the symptoms.

The exclusively organically oriented doctor may find himself in a predicament if the mother calls on him for help and he does not inform himself fully enough of the family situation and is not sufficiently cognizant of normal child development. Most general practitioners tend to await the outcome of "a touch of grippe," but the very ones who proceed most conscientiously may make mistakes here by giving less attention to the psychic problem than to the physical one. Since the prognosis in cases of fixed school phobia is unfavorable, the school phobia of this phase must be handled carefully, and misplaced physical intervention as well as coercion must be avoided.

It must be remembered that not all kindergarten teachers have pleasant personalities and that it may sometimes be necessary to place the child in another class. In my experience, however, such cases are exceptional. The child's difficulties in school, whether kindergarten or elementary school, usually originate at home.

If all goes well at the kindergarten, it is a really positive experience for the child, who finds pleasure in taking cognizance of reality. There is now in his life an authority whom he can place alongside his father and mother, and whom at first he often places above them. "Teacher says I should brush my teeth," he tells his mother, who has tried in vain to implant this idea in him; and she sees that Teacher's prestige achieves what she has not yet been able to achieve, for going to school is grown-up, and what Teacher says is thus grown-up. At other times the child discovers that he can turn against the grown-ups together with the other children, and that too is an important discovery.

If the kindergarten does not restrain his fantasy too severely, the child can greatly expand the limited environment of his home. For the first time he finds himself in surroundings with which his parents are less familiar than he is. For the first time he can tell about happenings that his father and mother have not experienced. For the first time, too, he notices that children are not all alike and that children are not all brought up in the same way—that some children, but not he, get angry and stamp their feet, that others can impulsively give away candy, which he does with such great difficulty. He notices also that there is a friendly but firm expectation of achievements which you can more easily get out of at home. Your coat belongs in one certain place and nowhere else, and you are expected to take it off and put it on yourself. If sewing cards seem babyish and you prefer to use your needle for something else, the teacher intervenes; you also notice that the other children sometimes turn in better performances, sometimes poorer ones. Building and measuring form a preliminary exercise for the later study of arithmetic. In short, the world has acquired a new dimension.

That not all is enrichment is noticed by the parents when the child's drawings suddenly become poorer. Sometimes the enrichment fails to please them, for example when the child's vocabulary is suddenly increased by a great many expressions which they do not approve of; or if the child suddenly discovers that children and grown-ups may also be considered each other's enemies. The contrast between the experiences gathered at home and in school may be a burden to the child. Generally the positive experiences at school win out.

*Readiness for grade school*

If the child is to be ready for grade school, the processes we have described in conjucntion with the decline of the Oedipus complex must have run their course in fairly normal fashion. If that is not the case, then the child is not yet able to set himself tasks and will have difficulty in bearing the burdens of school.

While the kindergarten can help to overcome the oedipal conflict, because the problem can be divided between teacher and mother, in grade school too much is demanded of the child's intellectual functions, and also the peer group is too large to be of help. That is, of course, not always true. Even the first-grader may speak of "the awful man the teacher's going to marry," because he himself, on account of his remaining oedipal feelings, wants to marry the teacher. Nevertheless it is true that on the whole the latency period must be reached before the child can deal with the subject matter of grade school, for otherwise there will be such complaints as "Plays too much," "Concentrates poorly," "Daydreams," and so on.

Together with growth in height and the eruption of the second set of teeth, we generally find psychic latency appearing. This is not always the case. Society stipulates, for economic reasons, that all children enter grade school at about the same age. Some, however, are ready half a year to a whole year earlier, others not until a year later; development, after all, cannot be measured by a yardstick. An extra year in kindergarten may then ward off a great deal of harm and give the child an opportunity to bring both his intellectual and his emotional development up to the latency level. It is the discrepancies between the two that lead to later disharmony. When intellectual development progresses but emotional development lags behind, this paves the way for later psychological disturbance.

In order to describe when a child is really ready for grade school, we must examine somewhat more closely the two forms of psychic functioning that Freud set side by side as the primary and secondary processes. In the infant every stimulus leads to immediate discharge, and only in the course of the first year does a delay in gratification become possible. The first principle, that of direct discharge, we call the pleasure principle; the other, in which delay of gratification is possible, we call the reality principle.

Very often gratification is possible only in fantasy, and this gives rise to magical thinking. The child, who feels so powerless, dependent, and small in the world of adults, compensates for this with unrestrained fantasies of grandeur. He is the king, the giant, the ogre of his dreams. Later he becomes an astronaut or a garbage collector, depending on which seems to him the more powerful. The testing of these fantasies against reality then constitutes another important part of the developmental process.

The earliest thinking is probably in the form of pictures, and just as in the very young child conflicting emotions do not yet subdue each other, so in this form of thinking there is no positive or negative, and contradictory ideas do not interfere with each other. As the child develops further, thinking becomes organized according to (1) cause and effect, (2) place, and (3) time.

From painful experience the young child quickly learns to avoid dangers in the outside world to some extent. Arrangement according to cause and effect makes its appearance. This is quite restricted at first and it is a long time before lasting belief in causality is established. The child's judgement is still often inadequate, so that he is prone to household accidents.

Together with an incipient feeling for cause and effect there emerges a limited ability for arrangement according to place; the child can find all the rooms in the house, and every spot has become familiar. Yet with most children it will still be some time before they recognize streets away from the immediate neighborhood of their house and learn to find their way. This differs greatly from one child to the other, but most leave it to their parents to find the way for a considerable time.

The last major organizational principle is according to time. Even when the child has been speaking in sentences for a while, time is still a difficult concept. "When I had my birthday tomorrow," says the four-year-old quite comfortably about the birthday that was celebrated the day before yesterday. There must, however, be a distinct beginning of this secondary process thinking before the child can accomplish anything in grade school.

Berta Bornstein was, in my opinion, right in saying that in the first half of the latency period the child pretends to think according to the secondary process while with companions of his own age he almost immediately reverts to thinking according to the primary process. I believe that this is an important point of view in determining school readiness, but I also believe that secondary-process thinking cannot really take place unless the oedipal phase has been to a large extent overcome. As long as the child remains dominated by instinctual conflicts, his logic is wrecked by them. In the transitional phase, in which the Oedipus complex is disintegrating, the child often develops a sort of philosophizing that is closely related to the philosophizing that makes its appearance in puberty as a means of dealing with instinctual conflicts. It is remarkable to see how this philosophizing is no longer manifested openly once latency sets in. The five-year-old is absorbed in speculations about the structure of life, about the hereafter, and asks those around him earnestly whether they believe in God; but the six-year-old needs all his attention for his racetrack, for his electric train, for the question how the flashlight is put together. The charm of this childhood philosophizing is that it is both naive and profound. The little boy answers the question, "Are you a cop or a robber?" with "I'm just kind of a plain man." "Do you believe that there's a God?" he asks, and, out of his wide experience, adds, "I don't think it's likely." So long as the child is absorbed in these philosophical speculations, he is not yet optimally adapted for school life. It is for this reason that I prefer the term "latency" for this period rather than "school age." Neither the beginning nor the end of latency coincides with what is called "grade school" in our culture. Fortunately latency generally begins earlier than the school age. However, it also ends earlier.

Here, in tabular form, I repeat the differences between primary-process and secondary-process thinking:

| *Primary Process* | *Secondary Process* |
| --- | --- |
| 1. Functioning according to the pleasure principle. | 1. Functioning according to the reality principle. |
| No delay of gratification possible. | Delay of gratification possible. |
| Discharge of impulses possibly with displacement. | Delay in discharge possible. |
| 2. Magical thinking in pictures. | 2. Logical thinking in words. |
| No articulation. | With articulation. |
| Displacement and condensation (one image representing different contents). | Causality recognized. |

| | |
|---|---|
| Contradictory ideas not mutually exclusive. | Contradictory ideas mutually exclusive. |
| No definite time sequence or location in space. | Organized in space and time. |

We must not forget that in dreams the primary process is dominant. But even in our waking life there is much more of the primary process in our thinking than we generally realize. Superstitions are a case in point. As soon as the emotions intrude, the ability to judge reality is diminished. A clear example of this is rumor and the influence it can wield. Another example is the stereotypes by which we judge those of our fellow men about whom we are not completely informed. They are convenient targets for all the hostility we cannot dispose of. Depending on our situation we need the Russians, the Chinese, the long-haired youths, parents, the establishment, on whom to discharge our hostility, in order to feel, in spite of our powerlessness in the face of world events, that we are able to form judgments about these events and thus be in command of them.

Naturally, no single change in life is as absolute as it appears to be, but it is undeniable that before the development of various functions there are susceptible periods, and that the beginning of latency is a particularly susceptible period for the development of the sense of reality.

If the child is to succeed in school, another requirement for school readiness must be met. He must have the inner freedom to attach himself to persons other than his parents Education can make fruitful use of the developing sense of reality. Concrete teaching enables the child to do what he is best adapted to at this age—namely, to take upon himself small, set tasks which he can carry out in accordance with reality. The Montessori method has been doing this more or less consistently for many year.

It is difficult at the moment to write about education, since the revision of teaching methods is in full swing. One thing is clear: teaching systems are relatively unimportant in comparison with the person of the teacher. Very different teaching methods can yield good results in the sense of completing a given curriculum. My own preference is for the Montessori method. There are also a great many children who can derive decided profit from the classical method, provided the teacher can unite the children in a positive orientation.

In the first grade, the Montessori method offers a great deal that is attractive. The child can follow his own tempo, he can do what is appropriate for his developmental level, and he can thereby reach a better understanding of his lessons and also more easily adjust to working together with other children without constantly diverging into a competitive position. If we compare this with the classical method, we can say of the latter that if such a group of small children is successfully made into a true group, the children will derive considerable support from it, naturally focusing on competition for the central figure, the teacher, who in these early grades is usually a woman. This collective rivalry over a woman leads to a return, in exceedingly moderated form, of the oedipal situation, which is useful in the resolution of its residues. The comradeship is then similar to that of siblings, and is based on the overcoming of rivalry. The Montessori class is based rather on the relationship between older siblings in the sense of mutual help; in this way children can overcome some part of sibling rivalry in play.

For pleasure in intellectual tasks, too, both methods have their own advantages. As I have already said, with the Montessori method it consists in being able to follow one's own individual path of development, whereas with the classical method it consists in being able to experience together with others the mastery of a specific intellectual difficulty—for example, the synthesis of a word out of the separate letters.

# 12 THE ACHIEVEMENTS OF THE YOUNG SCHOOLCHILD

Latency is typically the period in which the child develops a great many skills, in the intellectual field, in the motor field, and in the social field. Parents are often unhappy because interest in these skills does not arise of its own accord but is to a great extent oriented in the direction of their own interests. Sometimes they demand that the child show an interest in skills that they themselves do not possess.

In the early chapters of this book we have discussed how a child adopts from his parents what they offer him, how in the mutual cueing parent and child become adjusted to each other, and how the parents' offerings determine to an important extent the child's character development and his future options. Now, in the latency period, his interest in the spoken and written word will be influenced to a great extent by the way in which his mother has looked at pictures with him or whether or not she has read and told him stories. Whether books are valuable possessions in the family home or whether they do not even appear there is important for his future in school. The child who has become familiar with books and stories at home will in the first grade take great pleasure in discovering the combinations of letters that form meaningful words. If in the family home the news is brought only by television, the child will have much less interest in the written word.

In recent times more and more attention has been given to this arousing of interest in children who have not experienced it at home. But there is, to my mind, much too much emphasis on the sociocultural aspect and much too little on the emotional implications.

One of the unpleasant features of parenthood is that children seldom spontaneously take up anything for which the parents have little talent. A child must have tremendous musical talent to develop it in a family where no music is played or listened to. If he is to achieve anything in sports, he must spontaneously take great pleasure in motor activities if his parents do nothing more athletic than drive a car and know of sports only what they see on television. On the other hand, anything that is forcibly presented fails to reach the child; one can transmit only what one enjoys oneself.

In our type of society, exceptionally great value is attached to intellectual achievements, but a great many parents do not take pleasure in them. Parents who themselves do not enjoy intellectual pursuits demand of their children that they develop themselves intellectually. The businessman whose great strength lies in the skill with which he solves concrete problems and manages human relations expects his son to enjoy abstract mathematical problems; but the son does not enjoy these—he too takes pleasure in solving concrete problems, and he too has numerous friends with whom he has good times. That school performance suffers thereby is proof in itself that we overvalue intellectual achievements at the cost of all others.

What is true of the businessman's family is also true of the family of the uneducated workingman. If the family takes an interest in world events, the child will do the same. If such interest does not exist, its development in the child will be delayed.

What I wish to demonstrate here is that a lack of interest in school subjects cannot, in general, be treated as a problem of the so-called lower classes. Neglect of children occurs at all social levels. Sometimes this leads to learning disturbances, sometimes to impoverishment of the emotional life, sometimes to both.

Overstimulation also occurs frequently, perhaps more often than understimulation. If rapid progress in learning to read is overvalued, it can lead to reading disturbances, which are actually not disabilities but the result of a different tempo from that demanded at the cultural level of the parents. The emphasis on speed may give rise to secondary learning disturbances, which will be all the more severe if toilet training was also introduced too quickly and suddenly. The same parents who made too great demands then, will probably do the same now. In the mildest cases, in a child with great powers of assimilation, this will lead in both phases to a deconditioning of pleasure in the function; the resultant learning disturbances pass off with an improved approach.

But in many cases the child will internalize the conflict, so that both the parents' demands and the child's active and passive resistance to them are integrated into the personality and lead to serious character disturbances and a permanent aversion to learning. These cases can be handled only by means of psychoanalysis; but this takes us into territory that lies well outside that of normal development.

Within the framework of normal development it is important to know that, although the child in this period is able to make demands on himself and to carry out small tasks independently, he is still dependent on those around him. He is in constant need of the safe background afforded by the knowledge that his father and mother take a positive interest in his achievements. For a child who is called a grind if he does his best and stupid if he does not know things, learning becomes a bore. The same is true of children from families where quarrels are frequent. If a child, while in school, is preoccupied with thoughts of whether his parents are having a quarrel or of what sort of atmosphere he will find when he gets home, naturally that also has a depressive effect on school achievements. All serious family troubles—severe illness, death, separation—may disturb the learning process. But where conditions are favorable, where family relations are fairly normal, the child at school feels the secure background of his home, not only because he has learned in his own surroundings to approach other environments with confidence, but also because beyond the school there lies another dimension, anticipation of his return home.

Our school hours are rather long, and cause a good deal of tension which is released in noise when school is dismissed. In many young children one can also see clearly that they are tired by the end of the school day; they become restless, can no longer sit still, drop things, pummel each other under the desk, or leave school looking pale. They arrive home fretful, or hang around for a while first.

For most children the first need after school is something to eat or drink, and most mothers gladly oblige in order to renew contact with them. Now that such great, and particularly undiscriminating, emphasis is placed on the desirability of independence in children and the need for association with others of their age group, it can do no harm to point out to parents another desirable object—namely, to attach children to their home as well. In the first half of the latency period children certainly have great need of both. If the apartment is too small to invite children in to play, or if the mother is too worried about the neighbors, and if the street is too busy for playing, the child will surely lack contact with playmates. As a result, his ability to get along with playmates is not developed. But the child is also deprived in his relationship with his parents; for they are then no longer the secure background that he can fall back on after his wanderings, but grown-ups whom he has to deal with all the time—a compulsory association that is too much for both adults and child.

The schoolchild has far greater need than the two- or three-year-old of companionship outside the family, of friends of his own, even though these are still only friends for a very short time—companions for an hour, children to play with on the street. Emotionally healthy children make contacts easily and quickly, but these are still of a far from enduring nature. On the contrary, there may be a friend in the neighborhood, a friend at school, a friend at the day camp, and so on, without any of these friendships necessarily becoming permanent.

Sometimes it happens that both the children and their mothers are friends. This provides a certain stability, an expanded family bond that is beneficial to the children, insofar as it does not isolate them from other children. If parents try to insist on selecting friends for their children, their efforts will be in vain. Although lifelong friendships are generally made much later, the child's feelings about friendships between the ages of five and a half and eight years are much more personal than they were in the preceding period. It is undoubtedly a question of liking and compatibility, but not always of the same sort that the parents have in mind. Parents who cling to the ideal of their seven-and-a-half-year-old son as a husky little fellow may be shocked to find that he plays happily with the four-year-old boy next door and prefers to play little children's games. This can, however, indicate a relaxation in reaction against too stringent demands at home, and it falls well within normal limits. He bosses the neighbor's boy, just as his mother bosses him; and the neighbor's boy looks up to him, just as he has to look up, a bit too much, to his father.

I do not know why we ignore the fact that in this period the family remains the background for the child. Our one-sided emphasis on progress in school may account for this. In any case, it is my experience that even people who should know better very often fail to realize that the cause of disturbances in social relations is nearly always to be found in the family. Without a reasonably secure background there can be no free unfolding of social relations. Insecurity is, of course, just as likely to result from overprotection as from the lack of a secure home background.

The earliest learning takes place only by means of a personal bond to the teacher. There are teachers who cannot relate to a group of children, but more often it is the child who is unable to respond. This is especially so when the bond with the parents is so strong that the child cannot form the much less personal connection with an entire group of children. When there is a true neurotic development, a favorable outcome can be achieved only by treatment of both child and parents.

I have already written of children who are afraid to

go to school because there is great discord within the family. Children who witness quarrels involving physical assault between the parents are so uneasy over what may happen in their absence that they cannot remain calm in school. In these cases too, treatment of both child and parents is necessary.

Let me recapitulate what levels the child must reach in order to be able to go to school. First, there is height and the shedding of the milk teeth, an easy though inexact basis for judgment by the family doctor. Second, there is the decline of the Oedipus complex, which we cannot observe directly, and which therefore calls for a talk with the child. We can tell quite soon whether the child is still primarily involved with his parents or is now able to direct his interest outside the family as well—whether kindergarten is an important theme in his conversation or whether he thinks of it as an unpleasant interruption in his day with his mother. In the same talk we can then determine whether secondary-process thinking has replaced the primary process.

We should, then, start out from the following questions: Is the child able to carry out a small task? Can he follow instructions without much protest? Can he form grammatically constructed sentences that reflect logical thought? And finally, what is his attitude toward playmates—is he still unable to associate with others of his age group for more than a brief play period, or has he attained something approximating friendship?

One must not visualize these friendships too idealistically. They may well be coupled with a good deal of fighting. The only important question is whether there appears to be a certain continuity in the bond with other children. The children must be capable of coming together in groups, of forming ties with other children that will be strong enough to unite them in an orientation toward the teacher. If they are not able to do this, they become a disturbing element in school, since they will, for example, as a result of unresolved oedipal conflicts claim all attention for themselves, treat other children exclusively as rivals, destroy their work, and so on.

I should like to point out once more that failure to attain school readiness at the age of six years does not necessarily indicate a real developmental disturbance. There are, of course, among those children who do not reach school readiness at the age of six a certain number who will later develop a neurosis or a still more serious disturbance, but there are a great many more with whom it is merely a matter of a somewhat delayed emotional development. With this last group one may prevent an intensive negative conditioning by not yet exposing them to school life, for they have not yet grown up to it. Happily, this can be done. But unfortunately the reverse is much more difficult—namely, to place in grade school a child who has actually reached latency at the age of five. If this cannot be done, it means boredom in kindergarten and indifference toward schoolmates for precisely those gifted, overactive children whose development is progressing harmoniously.

I am definitely not an advocate of stimulating intellectual development at all cost, but neither does it benefit character development if the child no longer has enough to do in kindergarten and does not find enough stimulation there for the formation of his personality. The age at which a child may be admitted to kindergarten or to the first grade should actually be determined, not by socioeconomic considerations, but on the basis of the child's developmental level. He may be ready for kindergarten at three and a half and for the first grade at five and a half, but it is also possible that he may not yet be ready for kindergarten at five or for the first grade at six and a half.

In emphasizing the family's influence on the child I certainly do not intend to belittle that of the teacher and of the group. A teacher who understands the six-year-old, who knows how to make use of his desire to be occupied in motor activities—who does not consider running about the classroom punishable, but uses it as a basis for some small assignment—and who is prepared to experience a number of things with her pupils every day, offers a bit of security that may compensate somewhat for insecurity at home. But this can occur only if the insecurity at home is not too great. It makes a tremendous difference to children whether the teacher understands them and likes them or whether she carries out her duties reluctantly. A good atmosphere in a class signifies an expansion of the ego, a great reinforcement of the child's self-esteem, because he now proudly discovers that he can function in a group, and also because he derives from the identification with the teacher and the other pupils an enlargement of himself.

This group experience goes beyond the group events that the child encounters at home, since in the family the emotions are so much more closely involved. The school, being a neutral environment, can make the child realize how delightful it is to work at a task together with others. The certainty of being a good pupil can strengthen the child in his social role and increase his self-esteem.

This is particularly successful if the first-grade teacher finds ways of making a marvel of each day, thereby utilizing the dramatic sense of her pupils. This can be done only if she herself finds it exciting and goes about it in a natural way. Children are exciting, and six-year-olds are particularly so. Their feelings are expressed in their entire being; they come in at a gallop, and they disappear at a gallop. They are directly involved with the teacher and must pour forth everything that happens at home, insofar as it is not too emotion-laden. They all want to tell their stories at the same time, but it is much more than story telling—it is a matter of being close to the teacher.

The new subject matter is naturally full of difficulties; how can you tell the difference between *a, b* and *d?* Symmetry, in particular, plays tricks on children, and letter substitution and letter reversal may easily occur. Nevertheless, the recognition of the word under a picture, the recognition of a particular pattern, can give great satisfaction.

Of course, much depends on preliminary practice in the family. The child who has worked puzzles, who has built detailed structures, the girl who has repeatedly used the sequence red, yellow, green, blue for a pretty necklace, who knows how to mix two or three colors in painting, will much more easily learn to count and to express quantities in numbers than a child who has not had such practice because he lacked the play materials. A child with astigmatism, with faulty depth perception, or who sees with only one eye, will probably have greater difficulty with eye-hand coordination; he may, however, completely compensate for this defect. But in any case the child with poor eye-hand coordination will adapt less easily to the preliminary practice for arithmetic.

A well-conducted school provides an ego reinforcement not only because the child learns all sorts of new things, but because everything that is newly learned means an expansion. But there is also a feeling of satisfaction, of contentment with oneself, and of belonging to a group—a group that functions properly with a leader.

If all goes well, a child will look upon the teacher, not exclusively as an authority, but also as an ideal. To translate their diffuse feeling into technical terms: "We as a class, we children with a teacher, we form a functional group." It is absurd to think of the school as the natural enemy of the child, though both children and adults sometimes seem to see it that way. Rivalries and disappointments occur, of course, just as in other working communities; it is the school's task to help the child tolerate these feelings in limited doses. Unfortunately the dosage is often too great; but if all goes well, the result is not only a broadening of the ego, but also, above all, a broadening of the ego ideal. It is pleasant to achieve; it is pleasant to be socially integrated. In this respect the school is still a preparation for adjustment to society. And the adjustment that comes about in this way is not conformity, but independent functioning.

It is regrettable that our teachers are not systematically trained to keep their personal difficulties outside the classroom. On the contrary, such training is excessively meager, and this is the more serious since the teacher occupies a key position in relation to mental hygiene. The teacher who sneers at the slow child may erect a permanent barrier to learning. The teacher who views the group of children before her as her natural enemy spoils not only her own life but also that of her pupils. The teacher who is convinced that she can straighten things out with difficult Johnny but who drops the child if she is unsuccessful does not merely produce a disappointment for herself. She may not even see it as a disappointment but may talk about how impossible Johnny's parents are or how impossible Johnny himself is. The process will then be repeated with a later Johnny or Billy, to the great detriment of the children entrusted to her care.

I believe that if we want to improve education, a very useful starting point can be found here. A teacher who is fond of children, but only to satisfy her desire for power through them, a teacher who can impart a great deal of knowledge to the children, but only to achieve her ambition via the class, and who in doing so rides rough-shod over the incompetence of the less gifted, is for certain children a serious obstacle on the road to mental health.

In contrast, there are the many dedicated **teachers** who can unite the children around them and can inspire them, which is of immeasurable importance especially in the lower grades. Throughout elementary school and even the major part of junior and senior high school, the will to learn is present only if the bond with the teacher is strong enough and if the teacher can transmit the subject matter as an adventure in the exploration of the world. The teacher of the lower grades must have an understanding of the drama that life holds for a child of six or seven. The reason why life is so dramatic is that the child is for the first time encountering it with his individual ego and his individual conscience. In his early years his life has been determined in large measure by his parents; from now on he will take it more and more into his own hands.

Such a transition, of course, does not occur abruptly.

I have tried to make clear how in the first three years of life the child's ability to distinguish between himself and the outer world comes into being. The child has now acquired another function: he wants to judge for himself, or at least help to judge, what he considers good and bad. He still does this only to a limited extent; that is, he usually knows quite well what is right and what is wrong, but in practice he can apply his knowledge only in part, for he is still testing his own authority.

This sounds more complicated than it is. Most parents know that a child is happy to run an errand. But the child still needs considerable help in this, for the temptation of the candy bar or the toy may suddenly become stronger than the honesty that he has learned at home. Honesty has also doubtless become a part of his own conscience and a demand that he makes on himself—but the demand may weaken in conflict with the impulse to obtain what is so enticingly displayed. Sometimes these little pilferings are intentional expressions of resistance against grown-ups, a pleasant naughtiness with a display of courage—which is another kind of ideal.

It is no simple matter for a child to have to cope with so many different ideals. In the morality of the street, for example, daring is more important than anything else: "Have you got the nerve to swipe a candy bar, or haven't you?" Lack of daring is morally reprehensible on the street. At home, on the other hand, it is morally reprehensible to swipe a candy bar; your mother will ask you how you came to do such a thing—without histrionics if she is wise, and if she is unwise, then with horror or with concealed pleasure. The school has still another morality, which is usually stricter than the family morality: at school it is shocking if you have "found" a penny, or if you have taken a piece of the teacher's chalk from the ledge of the blackboard, whereas at home it is taken for granted that if there is chalk it is for the children.

Thus the child lives in a chaotic world in which he must feel his way along and in which he can find his way only if he feels secure both at home and in school. A child who has to go to school dressed differently from the rest feels trapped and conspicuous; a child who enters the class a few weeks after the term has begun has a more difficult time of it for this reason alone. On the street, too, a child who for one reason or another does not fit into the setting of the other children is out of step with them; a child who is not quite good enough, or just a little too good, at name-calling comes out the loser.

A low rank in the pecking order can be bettered, but not if neurotic motivations are involved. With normal children a small success, or a success in a particular field—a treat for the others, an outing with the class—may be enough to improve his status. If a child is always at the low end of the totem pole, in school as well as on the street, there is reason for anxiety and for careful investigation.

In school, of course, intellectual capacity is also a factor. A child who cannot perform a single task properly and yet must keep on in the school pattern has a particularly difficult time in the ordinary grade school. He has simply become a second-class citizen in the group, unless there is some other field in which he shines or unless the teacher can find a way of compensating him for his poor achievement—something that in my opinion occurs much more seldom than it should.

This problem could be met in part by reducing the

pupil load. One cannot expect of constantly overworked teachers that they take an interest in each individual child. On the contrary, one may be content if they work reasonably well with the group and do not cause too much harm to the children. Disturbing the atmosphere of the class as a whole has a more far-reaching effect than an incident with one child separately. If the wrong approach by the teacher is an extension of the errors in upbringing at home, even more harm is done. Essentially, a child—particularly a child in the first half of the latency period—can learn only if there is a positive bond with the teacher, and it is just the less gifted child who is most in need of this bond. By "less gifted" I am referring here to cases which still fall well within the limits of normal development.

There is a wide range of intelligence in the children of a single school class. The less gifted a child is, the greater is his need of concrete rather than exclusively verbal instruction. But the need for practice is also greater. At times these two factors are in conflict. A method of teaching arithmetic that is based on doing, that utilizes sticks and blocks to present the idea of quantities visually, requires a great deal of time and leaves less time available for practice. A method of teaching arithmetic that depends entirely on the mathematical symbols gives less insight but leaves much more room for practice.

We have already discussed the differences between the primary and secondary processes. Whether a child can handle arithmetic and language symbols easily depends, among other things, on whether the secondary process has become properly established. This is one of the factors on which intelligence is based. Another, and very important, factor is common sense. We sometimes see that children from whom reality is concealed—children who are not properly enlightened about sex at the preschool age, children who are not informed about family circumstances and, for example, are not told whether they are their parents' own children or have been adopted—fail completely in just this aspect of thinking. Such children adjust very poorly to school in spite of a high intelligence level as established by psychological tests. In these cases it is diagnostically important if a discrepancy is found, in an intelligence test, between a good score for abstract logical thinking and a poor score on the common-sense questions—a configuration that often occurs, especially in the case of neurotic children. With the less gifted the situation is reversed. At least, if they are properly brought up, their common sense may be reasonably well developed and abstract logical thinking, on the other hand, poor.

When the possibility of treating childhood neuroses is limited, it may happen that the I.Q. becomes lower with the passage of years. Slow children also drop farther behind in the long rum, but in the case of some neurotic or neglected children there is actual retrogression in the ability to use the intelligence, so that the ability itself can no longer appear in the test situation. It is strange that a society which attaches such high value to intellectual capacity gives it so little protection. In correcting this situation, both improvement in the mental health attitude of the school and earlier recourse to psychiatric help are important.

# 13 BASIC MISUNDERSTANDINGS BETWEEN PARENTS AND SCHOOLCHILDREN

We have already seen that adults can easily over-estimate a child's ability for logical thinking. But there are few parents who complain of this. A number of parental complaints, however, are so common that it is appropriate to mention them in connection with normal development.

The mother finds that her life is largely determined by the child's rhythm. She sees to his lunch when he gets home at noon, and she is at home when he gets out of school. The child, on the other hand, finds that his rhythm is completely determined by adults. They decide at what time school lets out; his mother decides whether he may go out and play afterward. This means that some resistance develops even in the kindest and soundest upbringing, a resistance that is expressed sometimes directly, sometimes indirectly. The child may get home later than he said he would; when he does get home, he may drop everything in the hallway and immediately run out again.

This last especially is a frequent complaint of mothers, who carefully plan their day so that they will be available when the child gets home from school. The child does not seem to appreciate this at all; he runs off, he goes along with a friend, he uses his mother only as the source of a snack and beyond this goes his own way. If his mother feels offended and wants to retaliate, she will see to it that she is not at home the next time. But then the child is deeply disappointed and offended, for just at the moment of his return he needs his mother, even though he treats her nonchalantly. For all day long he has had to make great—sometimes too great—demands upon himself, not so much in the way of intellectual exertions as in self-control in relation to the class, and when he is released from his imprisonment his first need is to make a racket and a mess. If his mother is not there to welcome him, even though she only says, "Hang your coat up," or something of the sort, he feels he has had no appreciation for the whole day's self-control.

But if his mother asks, "How was school?" the child answers, "Oh, O.K." or "Same as usual." Her question is seldom answered with detailed accounts; these come only later and in a very fragmentary fashion—in shreds as they occur to him at the table, while undressing, or at other odd moments, but not at the time when he gets home from school and wants to forget about it as quickly as possible.

Nearly all parents complain that the child never tells them anything about school, parties, or sports. They stay home to welcome their children, but the children do not seem to set any store by this.

The parents' great interest in the school makes the child feel that they care only about good grades and not about him. Sometimes this is a continuation of the feeling that they are loved only for being good, about which I have already written in connection with toilet training.

Another matter that troubles practically all parents is the fact that children get bored from time to time. Some children have more difficulty with this than others. A child in the preschool or latency stage who is often bored gives evidence thereby of a neurotic symptom. But all children are bored occasionally. Now, there are situations in which a child cannot escape boredom. In school, for example, a child whose intellect is far below the class average and who, therefore, in a standard curriculum, must constantly reach beyond his powers, exert himself too greatly, will as a reaction experience boredom for long periods, when he gives up the attempt to follow the lesson. A child with high intelligence, on the other hand, will become bored with the repetition of the subject matter that urgently requires repetition for the rest of the class.

Boredom at home generally has a different cause. Either something has been forbidden, so that the child cannot do what he wants to and converts the frustration over this into boredom, or the child is struggling with an inner conflict that he cannot put into words—for example, a disturbed relationship with his parents which he is not yet able to overcome.

Such a disturbance may arise, for example, if parents, with kindly intent which appears to the child as condescension, make such exclamations as "How nicely he's doing that! How sweetly she did that!" That sort of boredom is easily recognized. No matter what is suggested to the child, nothing strikes a responsive chord. Only when he himself, after friendly encouragement or after being let alone for a time, once more makes an exciting discovery does he succeed in relieving the innter tension. He can do that if the adults have not become cross and he can thus see that the relationship has not been broken off on their side.

This sort of boredom has a provocative effect. The parent becomes irritated, and the child gets a scolding.

Perhaps he even feels a need for the scolding—perhaps he has guilt feelings about unconscious libidinous impulses. But in contrast to friendly encouragement, a scolding practically never clears up the situation, since the parent's anger awakens renewed hostility in the child.

The influence of the repression of a masturbation impulse on boredom will be discussed later. In connection with the basic misunderstandings between parents and child it is of importance only to note how difficult it is for parents to handle boredom. Sometimes it is a misinterpretation on the part of the parent. The mother who is hurrying to prepare dinner and sees her little son loafing around in the room says, "Boy, stop moping around!" when she really means, "When I've got so much to do, you might help me a little!" She forgets that after the meal she herself will pick up the paper or turn on the TV, for at the moment she has less need of pleasant diversion than her son when he has just become inactive after playing on the street.

Not every form of inactivity is boredom. On a small scale it is often comparable to the discomfort that the creative artist experiences in the sterile period that precedes the creation of a work of art. This may also occur in children. Sometimes the child needs a little time to get a new play idea, a period in which he is seemingly bored.

Another and frequently occurring misunderstanding concerns the command, "First finish what you've started." It takes a great deal of practice for the child to know which of his self-imposed tasks he can complete. A boy of eight can perhaps rig up a bell with a battery—but if he tries to build a radio, he gets stuck. A model airplane construction kit may demand an impossible degree of precision. Parents are annoyed by the mess that is left or consider the kit a waste of money. The spirit of enterprise, already lessened by disappointment, is further diminished by scoldings. The father forgets that the book he bought six months ago is still unread on the bookshelf, and the mother, at the moment when she commands, "First finish what you've started," fails to remember the yard goods she bought at a sale, which has been waiting for months to be made into a dress.

A child who long ago learned to tidy up cannot do this at a time when something he is making goes wrong. At best he shoves the stuff aside for "later," as his mother, for that matter, does with the dress goods. Even when the child fully completes his self-imposed task, there may easily remain what parents consider a mess. The result of his work remains there, even though his interest has long since disappeared. If a boy is occupied in making something, his work space sometimes remains covered with string, screws, and nuts for weeks. It seems senseless to me to clear it all away after every session. It may be a nuisance, but it is better to let everything lie until the project has really been completed.

# 14  THE ROLE OF MASTURBATION IN THE LATENCY PERIOD

I concluded my account of the decline of the Oedipus complex by saying that changes never take place so quickly and are never so complete as written descriptions would seem to imply. Most children do not give up masturbation entirely during latency, but now it is rather a diffuse playing with one's own body, as it was before the masturbation of the oedipal period set in. It is therefore, as Blos (1962) points out, more a regulation of tension, a means of comforting oneself, a part of the regulating mechanism, rather than a specific outlet for sexual sensations.

We have already seen how in the first half of the latency period play in great measure takes over the role of the fantasies that accompany the Oedipus complex. At the same time, however, fantasies continue to exist. Freed from direct physical release, they live on. They always persist to some extent, though in normal children not to a disturbing degree. Outbreaks of masturbation, even as a release of sexual tensions, whether still directed toward the parent or displaced onto other parent figures, are often experienced as distressing by the child in the latency period—distress that we shall encounter again after puberty, with the advent of adolescence.

The latency child often experiences masturbation as something strange, something that he does not understand, nor want altogether. Frequently the link between fantasy and masturbation is broken, so that the action takes place but the fantasy is suppressed, or vice versa—fantasies and daydreams appear without masturbation. If these fantasies color the entire daytime life, a disturbance in the course of latency is involved.

But outbreaks of masturbation do occur in all children. The more normally the child has come through the oedipal phase, the more easily he will get through these outbreaks. In complete contrast to oedipal masturbation, the masturbation of the latency period is usually kept deeply concealed and is not noticed even by the parents. If a child in this period continues to masturbate openly, there is nearly always something wrong.

While the child in the first half of latency is occupied with suppressing masturbation, the struggle normally wanes in the second half. The child can, as it were, more easily allow himself these outbreaks, since he feels himself farther removed from the oedipal phase and is more safely absorbed in school life. Not until prepuberty will the conflict over masturbation return.

J. Lampl-de Groot (1950) and others have pointed out that the way in which masturbation and the fantasies originally associated with it are dealt with has a great influence on character development. Increased self-confidence may result if the child succeeds in suppressing the masturbation. That self-confidence enables the child to enrich his personality in a number of ways and then develops independently of its original source.

In girls one sometimes sees the following development: In giving up masturbation, an important role is played by the feeling of deprivation at the lack of male genitals. This feeling is masked by pride at being able to give up masturbation, often with a feeling of triumph over the "dirty" or "babyish" boys who cannot accomplish this. Such a development may lead to ideas of moral superiority and a certain rigidity of character. If this adjustment to sexuality is not corrected in puberty, frigidity will ensue.

This brings us back to the fantasy life. Injured feelings caused by the parents often lead to the fantasy that Freud (1908) described as the family romance: "I'm not your child, but the child of a high placed person, a king and a queen." Sometimes it is reversed: "I'm a poor little foundling." Such a fantasy, which is never expressed, engenders a secondary influence, not only on the attitude toward the parents, but also on the structure of the inner life of the child. The feeling of being different from others, of being much more or much less, of being an exception, is strengthened thereby. Sometimes this promotes independence, but more often, apparently, it leads to isolation, to feeling unappreciated, with an unexpressed feeling of superiority.

There is a close link between these fantasies and sadomasochism. The girl who looks upon the suppression of masturbation as a moral triumph over boys may compensate in these fantasies for the lack of instinctual gratification. A very frequent fantasy in latency is that of the bad men who take you along and do terrible things to you. On inquiry the "terrible things" appear to be sadistic acts. This is where fantasies of grandeur come into their own, and guilt feelings are avoided: the other person makes the child his victim. Also, the humiliating admission that the victory over masturbation is not so absolute after all is avoided.

These fantasies are, of course, reinforced by parental warnings against going anywhere with strange men, but they are not caused by them. In children who have really been exposed to sadistic acts one sees an entirely differ-ent effect—for example, in the form of an extremely limited, timorous, and depressed marginal existence with a great deal of suspicion and fear.

Fantasies of graudeur, even in these sadomasochistic forms, are not in themselves pathological. The little girl, a moment later, again derives her self-esteem from mastering roller-skating or from emerging victorious from a fight with her brother. But if the martyrdom or other sadomasochistic fantasies of grandeur form the core of self-esteem, there is definite pathological development that requires urgent treatment.

The great difficulty, however, is that these fantasies remain concealed: no one knows of them except the child. The parents find their little daughter, at most, somewhat too reserved, too docile, too lacking in spon-taneity, or they notice nocturnal anxiety—although even this last symptom is often kept concealed during latency.

# 15 THE SECOND HALF OF
## THE LATENCY PERIOD

In the second half of the latency period, logical thought develops to a much greater extent than in the first half. Moreover, groups outside the family become really important for the child. He goes on school trips, he goes camping under leadership, he goes out with friends, and he no longer needs the constant close bond with his family. He can now make overnight visits by himself and feel quite comfortable about it.

Belonging to groups—but still under leadership—is very meaningful to the child. The group focuses around the leader. In this way the child can enjoy group life fully, and can now and then join with the others in turning against the leader and thus discover that there can be conflicts that do not necessarily lead to a real break in the relationship.

This third milieu, that of the group, whether it be a scouting group or a club, plays an important role in the life of the latency child. If there are no organized groups, he will join a group of neighborhood children under the leadership of another child. The essence of all these groups is that they are centered on particular activities. A manual-training teacher can unite generation after generation of children around him; a gym group can provide great satisfaction for a large number of children. There are children who can make very little use of such groups, either because their parents take no interest in these activities or because they themselves are too closely tied to the home. There are also children who are over-burdened, who go from one group to another and are occupied with a group every day. Participating in different groups makes this still more tiring.

In my opinion, three groups a week are more than enough for a child. The golden mean is, of course, different for each child and is also greatly dependent on what the family itself has to offer. The allocation of the remaining free time is also shifted in part from the home to playmates.

In many families the question is properly asked, how much of their free time parents should spend with their children and how much free time children and parents should spend apart from one another. At the beginning of the first half of latency the child spends practically all of his time with the family; thereafter he spends more and more of it outside the family sphere.

## Interaction

The need for conformity with the age group certainly increases rather than diminishes, and it expresses itself not alone in the type of clothing worn, which will also play such an important role in the puberal period, but even more in behavior. There is great conformity of behavior in class, which is manifested in a regulated school life or in alignment with peers against adults.

Conformity may also be manifested in uniting with the school against another school, or in alignment with a group against another group, perhaps in the adoption of the parents' ideologies or of the school's outlook on life, or perhaps in the organization of secret gangs. By this I mean, of course, not delinquent gangs but those wonderful secret clubs that provide so much pleasure for eight- to ten-year-olds, the creation of a secret language, the guarding of treasures, the creation of private codes.

The child can now also, thanks to the development of abstract thinking, become proficient in such games as chess, checkers, Monopoly, and so on. The pursuit games do not, of course, die out all at once, but are partly replaced by sports, such as football, that are more subject to rules. If, in the preceding period, the child has learned to swim under the tutelage of his father or mother, he may now join a swimming class and earn a swimming certificate. Perhaps he will now learn to ride horseback.

Although the schoolchild now finds a large part of his gratification outside the family, he nevertheless arrives at a much more personal and realistic relationship with his father and mother. As he becomes more independent, the child now reacts to their personalities and their conduct, and not exclusively to their parental image. If his relations with them are good, the child is now affectionate of his own accord. He makes his own contribution to the family as a whole. When he becomes angry, there is a basis for it—and even in the most harmonious family there are occasional clashes. These disturb relations only if the parents fail to respect the child's independence—if they arbitrarily impose their will on him in a way that is not suitable for his age. If they are too anxious to keep the family together and do not allow their child the clubs or lessons or friends that now play such a major role in his life, he will rebel. The child needs a much greater measure of autonomy. He must decide for himself what he will wear and is miserably unhappy if his parents force him to wear clothes that are not in conformity with what the others in school are wearing, or that the child himself does not like for one reason or another.

In the latter half of latency, the child's increased rationality and autonomy, within the limits of school life, group life, and circle of friends, make him seem rather staid. He is very much the conformist. Fortunately, this conformity alternates with liveliness, roughhousing, and making noise. Parents find this annoying because it does not fit in with their own tempo, and may forbid behavior that is appropriate for the child. The prohibition then gives rise to disobedience, which they quickly interpret as unmanageability. But that is not the most disquieting behavior at this age level. On the contrary, it is the docile, withdrawn, quiet, and rather lonely child who is in greatest danger during this period. For if activity does not come into play at this time, it is very likely that it will never do so and that there will be learning difficulties and inhibition of creativity.

Later, the child in the second half of latency has conflicts with the parents about ordinary, realistic matters. For example, the boy uses his father's tools without first asking permission and without putting them away afterward; the girl insists that her mother get her dress ready today, although her mother has other things to do. The children refuse to help clear the table and wash the dishes, which the parents consider communal family duties.

Such commonplace conflict is part of normal growth, of learning to hold one's own, or marking out one's own territory, or learning to consider the rights of others. They are a sign of normal development. They do, however, lead to misunderstandings if parents are intolerant of ordinary misbehavior or interpret it as being pathological.

# 16 ADOLESCENCE

While the course of the developmental pattern in the infant can be described with relative ease, this becomes increasingly more difficult as the child acquires an individual personality. Thus generalizations become less universally applicable, even though the developmental pattern can be traced.

This is especially true of adolescence, for in this period the individual must find his own identity. There are so many ways of reaching that goal, and so many side roads that do not lead to it, that it is impossible to outline a universally applicable developmental pattern for adolescence. The danger of generalizations, based on limited observations, is nowhere so great as here

I shall restrict myself to a few broad outlines and must leave a great deal undiscussed. In this chapter, more than in any other in this book, what is said about "the child" or "the adolescent" cannot be applied to every individual child or adolescent. Moreover, adolescence is the period whose course is most influenced by the cultural environment. It makes a big difference whether at the beginning of puberty the child has already begun working life or whether he is still going to school. It also makes a big difference whether the adolescent sees all advertising addressed to him as the idol of the consumer society or whether, as a member of a minority group, he feels passed over.

Furthermore, the course of adolescence can be described only within a given culture and for a relatively short time. Cultural revolutions may do away with adolescence or, in certain cultural circumstances, prolong it.

When we consider the patriarchal family of the early industrial period in the nineteenth century, we can distinguish two types: ones in which adolescence was endlessly prolonged—namely, until the father relinquished control of the family business—and one in which adolescence was foreshortened because the child of ten or twelve was already working more than twelve hours a day in a factory.

In our culture, too, adolescence takes a different course at various levels. This is a field in which the psychiatrist must be very careful not to allow himself to be intimidated by the demands of society—demands that may expect him to treat as abnormal certain aspects of adolescence that to him fall within the norm, or to look upon certain abnormalities as normal, or at least not to relate them to their causes, since the causes form part of the culture.

I am thinking, for example, of constant intellectual overburdening. The lengthening of the period of compulsory education, however desirable it may be, makes sense only if education is really adapted to the pupils. Hypochondriacal complaints and conversion symptoms are often the result of intellectual overburdening. They provide a ready neurotic means of escape for the child who does not dare admit to himself his inability to follow the classwork. Children's guardians, teachers, school social workers, school doctors, and educators in the third milieu must keep in mind that truancy and minor forms of delinquency are also frequently the result of a too heavy school curriculum.

On the other hand, certain forms of behavior which,

in essence, may pertain to the normal process of adolescence, but nevertheless pose danger for the individual, are sometimes singled out by the media as typical. Thus we have here a terrain full of pitfalls, of which no integral description can be given.

Everyone who comes into professional contact with adolescents finds it difficult to view the behavior of the pubertal period from any point of view other than his own social level. What is normal in one section of the population may be abnormal in another. Above all, an understanding of the rapidly changing subcultures is important, but difficult to acquire. There are environments in which it is considered normal for sexual contact to take place as early as the thirteenth or fourteenth year; there are other environments in which such behavior may be the expression of a serious problem. We are particularly critical of others for what we ourselves have overcome with difficulty or what we have never admitted to ourselves. As a result, it is hard for an adult to be tolerant of immaturity and to avoid using himself as a yardstick in his dealings with the young.

It is, however, a sign of an equally one-sided approach if one sees all youthful rebellion as a reaction to frustrations caused by jealous adults who, organized in society, in the Establishment, begrudge them their rights. People are jealous of one another—the young of the old and the old of the young—and jealousy is an important motive, but not the only one. At least as important in the puberal period is the finding of one's individual identity: for the adult, when the parental role has to be restructured in a totally different form; for the adolescent, when he must attempt to achieve his ultimate independence.

Two forms of behavior in puberty are repeatedly

given publicity. The first involves mass action—protests, demonstrations, riots. It is simplistic to see only rebellion in such activities; they are also an expression of solidarity and of a search for new norms. In mob action, guilt feelings are lessened and pleasurable release of aggression occurs. I shall quote two youths to illustrate the influence of antisocial ideals and of mob formation (Hamblett and Deverson, 1964):

Terry Carson: I feel right proud of myself when I can bash someone in. Shows I can look after myself, that I have the strength and power to do someone over when other people haven't.

At a rough guess I've done about 350 people, the majority for money, but some in gang fights. My mate and I used to fire at people's feet on the towpath just to scare them, although I'd use the gun on anyone if I had to. Got it from a mate in Notting Hill.

Tony Williams: I kicked in a few scooters and caused a disturbance here and there with my mates, larking around. We went into an arcade and there was some geezer walking along with a bag full of pennies from the machines. I grabbed it and tipped it upside down and then ran off. I really couldn't tell you why I do these things. I suppose it's a bit of a laugh.

I don't smash things us now so much as I used to. Once I smashed four telephones, threw bottles at a shop window and overturned a bubble car with my mates. It was the thing to do—I must have been a nut.

It's exciting when the coppers chase you. It's great, you keep on running down sidestreets. To think someone's after you, trying to catch you, is all right.

That bystanders at disturbances eagerly enter into this pleasure in aggression is shown by the great throngs of spectators that converge on them.

The other behavior that so strongly attracts attention involves a shift in the use of stimulants within the cultural pattern from alcohol and nicotine to marijuana and more dangerous substances such as amphetamines, L.S.D., and narcotics. In fact, what is involved here is a cultural symptom that, as such, is not necessarily related to a normal or abnormal development of the individual. Prohibition makes the use of drugs exciting for the young, but drug users are no longer a special group. A great many young people come into contact with drugs and sooner or later are faced with the decision whether or not to experiment with marijuana. For the very reason that something new in the cultural pattern is involved, they cannot rebel against the example of their parents, and they must solve the problem themselves. Many will probably try it once and not again. For those who have become alienated from their environment, however, the subculture constitutes a substitute unit, a group they can leave only if the unfolding of their identity continues. In this way adolescence may be prolonged far into what is officially considered adulthood. I recall, in this connection, that the average age of drug users is twenty-three years (van Dijk and Hulsman, 1970).

Ideological motivations, such as the protest against the lack of correlation between prosperity and well-being, may lead to an alternative subculture. All ideologies—and therefore these too—may be used to repudiate serious personal problems, but they do not in and of themselves belong to either normal or abnormal development.

116

The adolescent is in a transitional phase that is particularly well adapted to criticism of society. Just at this time, when he has detached himself from the norms of his environment and need not yet assume societal responsibility for his own norms, he may have a clearer insight into what needs to be changed (Settlage, 1970). That is not the same as knowing how he would really want this done, for such knowledge is often lacking. This revolutionary ardor may become rigid and then have a destructive effect on personality development or lead to destructive behavior. Or it may, on the other hand, lead to a constructive idealism. It may even—and this, in my opinion, is what unfortunately occurs most often—rapidly ebb into a conformism reminiscent of that of the latency period.

Parents have difficulty in understanding what they themselves have never experienced. They are too much concerned with their child's future to determine whether the new factor is something transient or perhaps the beginning of a warped development. We cannot expect of parents either the objectivity or the specialized knowledge necessary for making the distinction; even for the specialist this is an extremely difficult judgment to make. A normally harmonious family provides a secure background not only for the child, but also for the parents. Only confidence in their child, increasing through the years, can help them to overcome their anxiety about the new and the strange.

This brings us back to individual development.

In the American literature the entire period is called adolescence. I shall adhere to the European usage, which distinguishes three periods: prepuberty, puberty, and adolescence. Just as in all developmental phases, it is true here also that both onset and progress show great variation.

Some children are already definitely in prepuberty by the age of ten, while others at thirteen still show the characteristics of a child in latency. As a result, children in the sixth grade may be in very different developmental phases. For some children this may prove a great burden, and, in neurotic children, may lead to school phobia.

This is true to an even greater extent in the first year of junior high school. Here too the difference in developmental phases among the children in the class may hinder adjustment to school life. Neither parents nor teachers always take these wide variations sufficiently into account. Children may be found either infantile or precocious when their degree of maturity is still well within the normal range. Often the child's development takes a great forward stride when he enters junior high school. This, again, is an example of the fact that what is too difficult for one child may be stimulating for another.

There is one point of view from which prepuberty can be described jointly for boys and girls: In both sexes the entire early instinctual development is run through once more. But since the boy and the girl, if the latency period was untroubled, have in the meantime developed in the direction of male and female individuals, their reactions to these arising instinctual impulses differ. We should note that, while in the physical sense the boy's puberty comes to an end with the first emission of semen, and the girl's with the first menstruation, in the psychological sense these events often indicate the beginning of puberty.

There is scarcely a clear parallel to be drawn between

physical and psychological development. While physical infantilism may well be coupled with psychological infantilism, we also see prepuberal and puberal changes in children for whom there is as yet no question of physical puberty, and vice versa.

Planting (1961) points out—correctly, in my opinion —how easily delayed psychological development may retard secondary growth in boys—for example, that of the muscular system. In children who are too anxiety-ridden to make use of their bodies the muscles, of course, are less strongly developed. The whole confusion in designating the phases of adolescence mirrors the confusion that is characteristic of the period.

I shall limit myself here to a description of psychological puberty and leave all normal biological variations in the advent of puberty out of consideration.

### Prepuberty in boys

The boy who felt so much at home in his life as a schoolboy, who had his own friends and his own sphere of importance outside of school, loses these in part. He drops certain clubs. He may become untidy about his person and his surroundings. His table manners may deteriorate, improving only slightly when he eats in a restaurant with his parents. He is likely to be unapproachable in his relations with his parents, especially his mother. It is as if, when instinctual impulses arise, the prepubescent boy is not so much driven to resist the impulse itself as he is unconsciously fearful that it may still be directed, as it was earlier, toward one of his parents. Insofar as early development is repeated, there is also a question of revival of the early dependence. Just as in early childhood he holds his mother responsible for his going to school clean, something that he has taken care of by himself for a long time. He holds her responsible, but he resists all her promptings, with the result that he goes to school dirty.

In our culture dependence on the mother is, for a big boy, a dreadful thing. We condemn culturally something that is part of normal development, and this leads to symptoms that are troublesome for parents as well as prepubescents. Some mothers spontaneously react very sensibly to this by involving their children in some project, for example, in the preparation of some delicacy. They may be able to create the necessary closeness and distance with a light touch—but this cannot be expected of all parents. If the renewed focus on bodily care leads to reproach and coercion, and especially to the mother's dealing with the child's intimate physical requirements, serious problems will crop up.

Mutual contact between boys also becomes rougher, fighting more sadistic. Sometimes the sadistic impulses reach an intensity that is frightening to the child because of the rigidity of the defenses he has built up against them. If this conflict assumes major proportions, it may lead to paralysis of all initiative. The child moons around, partaking of no activity whatsoever—a symptom that parents often find very disquieting.

The boredom of latency often rests merely on a misunderstanding between parents and children. Parents, that is to say, expect activity of their children at a time that suits themselves. The boredom of prepuberty, however, points to a true intrapsychic process and has to do with the defense against libidinal and aggressive impulses. This defense is at times so strong that all initiative is obstructed.

While, on the one hand, the boy defends against instinctual impulses—certainly insofar as these are still directed toward his parents—sexual curiosity, on the other hand, increases enormously. Initially this curiosity, in accordance with the nature of the instinctual impulses, is directed toward cruelty, toward the anal and excretory functions. Quite soon, the genital is added, but exclusively as a bodily function, completely divorced from emotion. If the development of sexual life does not proceed further, we have the disturbance that Freud (1912) called "the universal tendency to debasement in the sphere of love." Although during latency the child, even if he has been properly enlightened, is often convinced that his parents don't do such things, children in prepuberty often think about their parents' sex life. But their thoughts are, just as in the preschool age, colored by their developmental phase. For the boy or girl who is still too much engrossed with anal impulses, thinking about sexual matters is equivalent to thinking about what is dirty and forbidden. Thus his parents become contemptible persons who do dirty things themselves but forbid him to do them.

It is remarkable how little change a shift in the cultural sphere brings about in these emotional adjustments determined by development. It makes a significant difference, of course, whether a child grows up in a family where the parents have a satisfying love life and are well adjusted to each other sexually. Development is hindered if just at this time of rebellious dependence, of increased dependence with rage because of it, the mother in her loneliness seeks more closeness with her son, or the father, because of his own lack of gratification, vigilantly spies on his son's budding instinctual life. But the culturally determined greater freedom in the sexual sphere brings little change in the child's developmental process.

The overvaluation of sexual enlightenment must once more be mentioned in this connection. It is certainly important to enlighten children, but if this still remains to be done in prepuberty, it is already much too late, and the parent runs the risk of rejection by the child. In this period the child is much more interested in finding out for himself. He no longer wants to be enlightened by an authority. The eleven-year-old may encounter an older friend who enlightens him, or someone in his peer group. He may search surreptitiously in his parents' bookcase or make use of the booklets that they have, with apparent casualness, left around for him. The reproach to parents, "You don't tell me anything," is there at the same time, but that reproach is perhaps more appropriate to actual puberty than to prepuberty, in which secrecy plays an important role for both sexes. In the second half of latency, too, secrecy certainly plays a role. The robbers' cave in which everything is kept, the secret plans, and the secret writing or secret language represent segregation from adults and a banding together with one another. In prepuberty secrecy acquires a much more distinctly sexual coloration. It is now a question of sexual knowledge, possibly of knowledge about masturbation.

Learning from one another to masturbate, discovering masturbation together, has practically nothing to do with homosexuality, but much more with anxiety about the masturbation that still occurs regularly.

Masturbation is experienced as tremendously exciting and fearsome at the same time. It is no wonder that an organ in which so many changes appear is regarded with admiration, but also with concern. When boys compare the size of their penises, this is completely within the normal pattern. It is important for the prepuberty boy because there are certainly others of his own age who either show hardly any physical changes as yet or have already arrived at complete physical maturity. The spontaneous movement of the penis, the increase and decrease in size, may revive the old castration anxiety.

Human beings are becoming taller, and physical sexual maturity begins earlier. As a result, the child has to cope with it at a time when he is still emotionally immature. It is understandable that many children, in spite of what they can read or see on television every day about sex, often face it with anxiety.

*Some aspects of male puberty*

The first emission does not necessarily occur in connection with sexual stimuli. Any sort of excitement may trigger it, perhaps roughhousing with friends, or the prospect of a school test, or other diffuse tensions. In this sense the emission acts as a regulator, as a release of tension, and not as a specifically sexual occurrence, as it will when the boy has reached psychological maturity. His attitude toward his sexual impulses at that time will depend, to a limited extent only, on the education and enlightenment that he has had. A boy may still be taken completely unawares by the emission (and a girl by the menarche), and at first think of it as abnormal. In my experience, however, this generally rests upon a preceding neurotic development, preventing the child from making use of opportunities for sexual enlightenment. But it may also be simply the result of the fact that the boy is psychologically still in the stage of prepuberty, and perceives the emission as a sort of incontinence.

If the first seminal discharge does not come as an unpleasant shock, there is a resurgence of activity and masturbation ensues. The masturbation fantasies are at first diffuse and not centered on a specific person. In the beginning the masturbation is often induced more by fantasies of grandeur than by direct sexual stimuli. But it is difficult to get enough information about this. Puberty boys are frank among themselves about these fantasies, but they do not confide them to adults.

In my opinion neither adequate enlightenment nor the intellectual knowledge that all boys masturbate dispels the guilt feelings about the first sexual fantasies. The nonappearance of guilt feelings is, to my mind, far more dependent on the developmental phase in which the masturbation occurs and on the degree to which the boy has inwardly detached himself from his parents. By this I mean not the resistance to his parents, but whether the libidinous fantasies have shifted away from the parents to others. If they have, one can say that masturbation has never been a problem and is experienced without complications or guilt feelings. On the other hand, there are violent guilt feelings brought on even by apparently harmless fantasies, if in the unconscious every woman, every girl, still represents the mother and if the excitement is connected with fantasies that are regarded as humiliating to the mother. The severity of the superego, which reached its development in latency, forbids indulgence in such fantasies. These then attach themselves to harmless figures, mostly strangers: a girl casually seen at a distance on a bicycle or at a movie. No attempts to make contact are undertaken. The fantasies are considered humiliating and embarrassing.

Secretly, certain of the mother's physical characteristics, which the child must not consciously criticize or even notice, foster the excitement. Thinking about the mother in physical terms is then experienced as absolutely forbidden. In this way the superego blocks the progress of instinctual life. Thus arises the paradoxical situation in which just because the conscience is so severe the true inward shift of the drive impulse from the mother to other women cannot come about. It constitutes a feedback system: fixation in the oedipal phase brings about the formation of an over strict superego, which in turn makes disengagement more difficult. If the oedipal fixations are not too strong, they may be broken down in the course of a favorable pubertal development, and this justifies the optimism of many educators.

The activity that the boy displays at the onset of puberty need by no means, of course, be an activity that is approved of by his parents. On the contrary, the need to suppress, to avoid all drive impulses toward the parents, often forces the boy to mobilize his protest in order to be able to deny his dependence more forcefully. His activities may then often be directed to a specific goal which is not highly appreciated by his parents. Often it is difficult to make it clear to parents that this activity is, after all, a part of normal development. But what in itself is perfectly normal is not always free from danger. There are certain activities—for example, the formation of delinquent gangs—which constitute a danger for future development, but which are nevertheless much more normal than a great many parents believe.

During puberty the disengagement process may lead

to difficulties because both the parents and the child are so closely involved in it. It often happens that the father really feels his dignity threatened by the boy and therefore resists long before there is any need for resistance.

Because of these problems the personal life of parents is even more troubled than during the child's preschool stage. When they have company in the evening, the boy joins the group, joins in the conversation, and leaves no doubt, in his tone of voice and choice of words, of his contempt for parents who talk inanities all evening. The parents feel that their child has rejected them and made fools of them, and they react to this after their fashion. And the evenings are long: children at this stage do not submit to being sent to bed. At best they have their own circle of friends, but then parents are annoyed that their company is no longer appreciated.

In order to see the criticisms of present-day youth and present-day parents in proper perspective, we may recall Balzac's description of the club of "les hommes de mauvaise volonte" (men of ill will) founded by young rebels living on the edge of Paris society. Dickens, in his characterization of the landlord of the Maypole (in *Barnaby Rudge*), gives a good description of a father who belittles his lively, intelligent son as a dolt. In essence this is a never-ending conflict. It is a matter of development of the adults as well as of the child. The parents derive part of their feeling of self-esteem from the way in which they bring up their children. As long as the child continues to develop favorably, parents are inclined to take this as their own achievement. If that feeling is too strong and if it is not coupled with full respect for the child's personality, more and more difficulties arise as the child grows older. A child does not want to be an achievement of his parents; he wants to feel that he is appreciated for himself. It is in their children's puberty that parents must learn to look for their feeling of self-esteem not in their children, but in their own manner of living. This process runs parallel to the disengagement process of the children. Just as the course of puberty is extremely important for the child's adult life, so the working through of the children's disengagement is important for the course of the parents' later life.

The pubescent's new activity may at first take on the character of a triumph over his father: "Dad is no good at winter sports; I can do things much faster; he can't do anything with his hands; I can do anything; Dad doesn't know anything about the new math."

Even if such activities are a form of bluff, this does not mean that they lose their importance for the child once disengagement has been fully accomplished. Sometimes he learns to take pleasure in the activity as such and, as an adolescent and an adult, continues to enjoy the pursuit of what has become his special field of interest, even though it is no longer needed for disengagement from the parents.

The same applies to the interest in space and distance which may serve in this period as a defense against immediate difficulties. Emotion may be so strenuously warded off in puberty that any breakthrough seems catastrophic. This prohibition against repression of emotion is the end product of the childhood wish for physical contact. The toddler was used to sitting on his father's or mother's lap; the puberty child feels so threatened by the wish to have such physical contact that even having an emotion, a feeling of rapport, is interpreted as a sort of physical contact and must be repressed. The stars in the sky, prehistoric animals, space travel then stir emotions that are connected not so much with the subject as with the warded-off conflict; but in the process a lifelong interest may well have been awakened. Even the philosophizing that serves to repress emotions during this phase may, when this service is no longer needed, lead to intellectual enrichment through the study of philosophy. The desire to be occupied with inanimate things rather than with forbidden, dangerous feelings and wishes toward living parents may stimulate the child to develop his mechanical skill.

These manifestations of activity are much more agreeable to parents than the nonconformist ones—all the more so because there is more protest and hostility incorporated in nonconformist behavior. Parties, drinking, flirting with girls, and smoking marijuana are types of behavior that often make parents uneasy. Yet they need not be an expression of abnormal pubertal development. It is the fact that so much of what occurs during puberty is abnormal in other life phases, or if it continues beyond puberty, that makes the diagnosis of behavior disturbances in this period so difficult.

### Prepuberty in girls

In the girl, prepuberty makes its presence known in a different manner from that in the boy. Often her boyishness increases to begin with. She refuses to recognize changes in her body and has a definite preference for boys' games. The anal regression that is prominent in the boy is less evident. There is a greater regression in identification with the mother. At this point she identifies less with her mother as a woman than with her mother as an industrious housewife. It is a period of being willing and able to do everything, which makes the transition to junior high school simpler for her than for the boy—at least, if she is at that time still in prepuberty and not in puberty. She is usually taller than boys of the same age, from which she derives a certain superiority.

For the girl, as for the boy, in the matter of sexuality the knowledge of bodily functions stands in the foreground during prepuberty, especially the rediscovery of sex differences as something secret, something strange, something to giggle about with friends. She may possibly pass notes about it, with the extra suspense about whether they will get to the teacher, a suspense that is always resolved pleasurably. If the note does not get to the teacher, the girl has the triumph of an undiscovered secret over the adults with their secrets. If it does get to the teacher, this may give the girl some very embarrassing moments, but she has the erotic, aggressive satisfaction of causing the teacher some worry. If the note is passed in a woman teacher's class, it expresses— besides the excitement over the secret—enmity toward the woman, which may be transferred from the relationship with the mother.

It is notable that girls sometimes revert to the role-playing of the three- to five-year-olds. Some girls of eleven or twelve still use dolls for this purpose; others stuff a pillow under their skirt and play at being pregnant, wear their mother's shoes, and so on. I have repeatedly heard from girls that their first sexual impulses to be revived were coupled with strong feelings of aversion to the father, in the form of a physical disgust. Just as parents complain about the bad table manners of their children, some prepubescents and pubescents complain about the bad table manners of their parents. The way the father slurps his soup or mashes up his potatoes may drive the girl to despair. To some extent she is using this means of taking revenge for earlier instructive remarks, but to a great extent this aversion replaces the aversion to her own libidinal impulses, which are still directed toward her father.

### Puberty in girls

The transition from prepuberty to puberty often occurs in conjunction with the menarche, which may cause a sudden change in the girl's frame of mind: on the one hand, she experiences the magical sense of being an adult, and on the other hand, fury. If she is psychologically still in prepuberty, she may experience the menarche as something dirty, as a sort of incontinence. Thus, regression to anality occurs just as in the boy, but somewhat later.

In the literature it is sometimes suggested that masturbation starts later in the girl than in the boy. I do not really know whether that is so. It may well be that under the influence of the dissatisfaction with her genitals, masturbation is sometimes almost completely suppressed, but here we enter the realm of pathological development.

As I see it, masturbation in girls leads rather to a dissociation, so that there is a less guilt and masturbation is regarded as something apart from everyday life. While the boy may brag to his friends about his masturbatory achievements, the girl is more secretive about it, seldom speaks of it, but nevertheless enjoys it thoroughly. As I have already said, it is extremely difficult to obtain reliable data on this matter. The gathering of exact data is made more difficult by the fact that pubertal experiences are often as deeply repressed as infantile development, so that there is no point in making inquiries.

In the girl, as in the boy, fantasies are often dissociated from masturbation. Sometimes there are conscious fantasies and dreams of the future. I have already described how little girls regard their genitals as a missing penis and temporarily feel they have been physically short-changed. If this feeling persists, it is sometimes reversed in puberty. The discovery that she is a good-looking girl who is attractive to boys leads to increased but unstable self-confidence. The curious feeling of invulnerability that is coupled with this become dangerous if it induces the girl to venture into social situations that she is inwardly unable to cope with. This may lead to hazardous behavior. One sometimes sees young girls behaving recklessly with a strange, triumphant half-smile. This half-smile betrays the inner constellation of being invulnerable in which the behavior originates. It is a form of play-acting, which we have mentioned as being typical in prepuberty.

Until well into puberty, there is an alternation between making herself attractive as a girl and suddenly reversing the pattern; typically both occur at the same time—for example, in the use of provocative makeup and the wearing of very conventional, dull clothes. Usually a number of short, temporary infatuations have to be suffered through, often at a distance; these are disclosed to girl friends as deep secrets and discussed with each girl friend as a new secret.

As with boys, there is an increased dependence on the mother, whom the girl must then resolutely keep at a distance. Anna Freud (1958) points out that what parents object to is not so much their children's independence as the complete reversal of roles. It often seems as if the girl really has to carry out the fantasy, "Later I'll be big and you'll be little," and has to make it quite clear to her mother that the latter is through as a woman. That mothers protest against this is understandable.

Some mothers, however, find it very difficult to watch their daughters blossoming out. On the one hand they are, naturally, extremely proud of their daughters, since nearly every healthy girl at this age has a certain charm; on the other hand, this same charm engenders rivalry. Furthermore, this pride may give rise to great resistance in the young girl or plunge her into confusion because her mother's excessive interest makes her feel that she must be successful for her mother's sake instead of for her own sake.

Esther Matthews (1969) rightly warns against the danger that vocational guidance counselors may give too much weight to a girl's choice of occupation based on a pubertal fantasy. This is one of the dangers of late maturing together with early choice of occupation; the combination may lead to choices that are determined by prepubertal adventurousness. The same is true in puberty, when the choice of occupation may be determined by glamour.

*The identity crisis in puberty and adolescence*

In the sixteenth or seventeenth year, puberty changes into adolescence. By then, there is sufficient emotional maturity for reintegration to make its appearance. The identity crisis that takes place in puberty becomes in adolescence a gradual quieting down, a reintegration, a finding of one's own role and status, of one's own nature, of one's perception of oneself. Along with this quieting down more stable self-esteem is established.

We have seen that biological puberty is often over just when psychological puberty begins—namely, at the time of the greatest disharmony in physical development. For that is the time when the first emission or menstruation occurs. For the child, however, all the changes in his body betoken an entirely different perception of himself. This is certainly not related to the physical changes exclusively, but nevertheless these play an important role in it. The adult forgets how he looked at himself in the mirror to see what changes had occurred, with the anxious feeling of "Am I still that, or am I really not that any more?" "Is that creature with the gangly legs and arms, the big hands and feet, the pimply face—is that the same creature that in grade school took pleasure in his own gymnastic skill, and in his own harmonious functioning?"

The pubescent does not fully realize that this disharmony is only temporary and that it will correct itself between the advent of sexual maturity and adulthood. But apart from that, even if he were completely aware of it, it is still an eerie feeling to find such changes in one's body. It is like Alice in Wonderland, who by turns is much too tall and much too small. "Who am I and what will become of me?"—that is the identity crisis every pubescent must go through in one form or another, perhaps in moderate form, perhaps protracted and turbulent.

The feeling of a personal inner continuity, the feeling

of remaining oneself, is diminished, and sometimes almost entirely destroyed, by the great changes in the body, but also by the increased intensity of the drive impulses and the change of social status. The surging drive impulses are not recognized by the adolescent as part of himself. He has the frightening feeling of having lost himself, of being another person. With the breaking away from the parents, not only the self-image, but the image of the world becomes muddled. The preschooler, and to a lesser degree the schoolchild, views himself very definitely as part of the family, in relation to his parents. When this feeling of belonging begins to recede, it is replaced by feelings of great loneliness, of being misunderstood not only by those around him, but also by himself.

This is reinforced by another phenomenon. With the resurgence of the oedipal emotions, the development of the conscience, which arose out of the decline of the Oedipus complex, also becomes unsettled. With the criticism of the parents those norms of theirs which have become internalized are more or less abandoned. The parents' ideals are no longer those of the adolescent. Their prohibitions are no longer heeded. All this leads to feelings of anxiety and loneliness, which are common in puberty and adolescence. As a reaction there arises great conformity within the peer group, a comfortable adoption of another's identity. Pinups of athletic heroes and movie stars may help to accomplish this, as may the playing of a favorite singer's records. But at the same time it is a matter of much more concrete, intensive mutual identifications among friends, much stronger than at any other age, with much more extensive adoption of specific forms of behavior. The need to have what the other has is no longer dictated exclusively by ordinary jealousy, but is a necessity of life for maintaining one's own personality. We have already seen with what difficulty feelings of dependence on the parents are dispelled. Quite often the identification with friends conceals a great dependence. Girl friends who have just said good-by, after they have spent the school day together, have hung around together during the lunch hour, have walked home together or sat together in the school bus, and then have stood at the door talking and finally have gone their separate ways, the moment they get home reach for the telephone to keep each other up to date on the latest complications with their parents, or merely to keep in contact. These are the same girls who are furious if their mothers criticize their behavior, or even ask with interest how things went at school.

The boy who arrives home after working hard all day must immediately go to the friend with whom he has worked so intensively, whether to do homework or, more pleasurably, to tinker with the setting up of an involved experiment. It is not that the experiment will prove anything or that the tinkering will really be successful; it is a matter of continuing the contact with the friend, to protect himself against the feelings of dependence at home, against the drive impulses that give him difficulties, against his mounting loneliness.

In such a friendship it is very difficult to mark the boundary between dependence and identification, for both, after all, stem from an earlier phase. Apart from that, such friendships may be a particularly promising beginning of permanent friendships. Anyone who is unable to form a friendship in puberty will usually find it difficult to do so in later life. But this does not mean that these pubertal friendships are always long-lived. Sometimes what started as identification or as the conquest of dependence may develop into an adult friendship in which the personalities of both will flourish. Even the finest friendship, however, does not relieve the feelings of loneliness that are bound up with the identity crisis in puberty.

The intensity of these processes differs enormously from case to case. Some young people continue their schoolchild existence, with hardly more than a ripple, up to adulthood; others go through a severe crisis with true mourning (Lampl-de Groot, 1960). Never does one feel so lonely as when one is no longer sure of one's identity.

The feelings of loneliness in puberty may arise from very different sources. One source is the identity crisis; another is the loosening of the ties to the parents, by means of which the most important personal relationships of childhood are lost from within. Above all, when the vestiges of dependency, or of the libidinal bond, or of primitive aggression must still be strongly suppressed, the loosening of these ties takes on a convulsive form in a complete turning away from the parents. Sometimes the partial disintegration which is part of the puberty crisis coincides with the height of the estrangement from the parents. The puberty child feels that he is not merely a stranger in the home, but a stranger to himself. He not only loses contact with his parents of today, but in rejecting old ideals and norms loses also the inner approval of the parents of former times.

Sometimes there is a distinct difference in phase and a certain independence toward the parents arises before the identity crisis has reached its height, or the pubescent finds support in the partial dissolution of superego and ego ideal by means of a still close family tie. But if the family crisis coincides with the identity crisis and the crisis in sexual identity, feelings of loneliness and rancor may be so strong that a dangerous situation results, with increased possibilities of suicide.

We have seen the physical changes of puberty as one of the causes of the identity crisis. The finding of sexual identity is a fundamental aspect. Doubt in the ability to function as a man or as a woman are inevitable. In this regard too the pubescent asks himself, "Who am I and what will become of me?"

"Will all the women fall in love with me?" asks the boy, "Or am I such a dud that I'll never be able to get a girl? Will I be an ardent lover? Or will it just be a question of one pleasant evening, and after that I'll want a different girl? Am I a homosexual because I masturbated with my friend?" And the girl wonders: "Do all the men look at me when I walk down the street? Will a boy ever fall in love with me? Am I a Lesbian because I sort of idolize my social studies teacher? Did my Spanish teacher not call on me because he knows I'm in love with him? Frank asked me for a date—does that mean that he can't get along without me? Shall I go to Mexico with John? Not a single boy today has asked me to that party; does that mean that I'm no longer attractive?"

One's self-esteem as man or woman is consequent to one's entire development from early childhood to adolescence. In adolescence the important thing is to gain confidence in one's own sexual role. This is successful only if the preceding phases have been gone through reasonably well.

I have already described how young girls may for a time consider themselves not only good-looking but invulnerable. A comparable phenomenon in a young man is the temporary overrating of the penis and of potency. Sexual experimentation while masturbating then takes place in front of a mirror, and the fantasies concern limitless potency. Transitory contact with girls is then characterized by Don Juan fantasies and not by sex play, in which the perception of the other person also plays a role. It is as if self-esteem depended on sexual achievement and must constantly be reestablished. This often alternates with hypochondriacal complaints, in the course of which anxiety about the overrated organ becomes evident. If such a development takes on a serious form, it is a pathologic regulation of self-esteem (Reich, 1960). In milder cases it may be part of normal puberty and may lead, by means of the many experiences with girls, to genuine contact.

Not all boys have a need to experiment. There are a good many who achieve a true choice of a partner quite early, though this need not yet be permanent. I mean by this that the relationship with the girl is a truly personal one, even though such love affairs often fade out. This is true for the girl as well as for the boy. The passing of such a love affair then causes the feelings of loneliness to flare up violently again. Just as an unhappy marriage may jog along because both parties are afraid to be on their own for a time, so a love affair may be prolonged by fear of loneliness, especially if one of the two clings to the relationship tenaciously. Usually a new love affair on the part of one of the two puts an end to the relationship. The other then feels deserted. Such grief is no less intense than that which follows the breakup of a marriage, but fortunately it is generally of much shorter duration.

Persistent unhappy love may be considered a

pathologic phenomenon (de Levita, 1967). It is the lack of self-esteem that makes it impossible to abandon the unreal attachment to the unattainable girl. Generally it is not only the girl who is involved, but also her parents—another indication that the adolescent has not succeeded in detaching himself completely from the parent figures. Such a persistent unhappy love embitters the adolescent's life not only through the distress it causes but also through the further undermining of self-esteem and through loneliness in relation to the peer group, where the other boys have girls. Normally the distress, however unpleasant it may be at the time, contributes to the adolescent's realization of his own identity, and often a following relationship is of a more permanent nature.

Still another normal outcome is possible—namely, that the first love affair develops into an enduring relationship that actually leads to marriage. The partners then go through a part of the development to adulthood together.

Usually the choice of an occupation comes about before the choice of a partner, for the former has been partly determined by previous schooling. The adolescent who goes to work at the age of fifteen or sixteen has not yet, it is true, found his groove, but he often follows a definite trade. Only for those who pursue higher education is it true that the choice of a partner precedes entry into an occupation, but even in these cases the nature of the future occupation has already been decided.

If both the choice of a partner and the choice of an occupation have been made, even though there may as yet be no marriage or education has not been completed, adolescence has come to an end. After that we speak of adulthood. This does not mean that growth has also come to an end. I hope, for example, that I have described, between the lines, something of the growth processes in parents; similar growth processes appear, if all goes well, in every sphere of life. It is in the very nature of a successful adolescence that new personality adjustments come into being, not according to rigid patterns established in early youth, but according to current reality.

*Sublimation—hobbies—creativity*

We have already seen how, with the decline of the Oedipus complex, intellectual curiosity grows out of sexual curiosity. During puberty sexual curiosity again plays an important role and intellectual curiosity is once more directed entirely or primarily to sexual questions or simply bodily functions. Eventually, however, a large proportion of intellectual curiosity no longer has anything to do with sexuality as such. This is quite clear in latency, when the child's wide interests so often astonish parents. In prepuberty the drives flare up strongly again in the desire to know, and in puberty we note that there is a revival of curiosity, in a form that may now have become permanent; it is no longer attached to sexuality, but takes the form of interest in the outside world.

During adolescence, however, it is difficult to form a judgment on this point. A great deal of the broadened interest is held together by the revival of the drives and seems also to be linked to their flowering, so that once a satisfying adult sexual life has come into being, this "luxury" energy wanes and the basis of interest becomes much narrower. In adolescence we can hardly judge to what extent interests will endure. This applies particularly to creativity, which is usually keener in the preschool period and in early latency than in the second half of latency, and is revived at the beginning of adolescence—that is, in the second phase of puberty—and sometimes leads to remarkable achievements.

The early loves may be particularly inspiring; anyone who does not write poetry, paint, or play or compose music in this period will probably never do so. If we interpret "creativity" in its broadest sense, that of "making" something, being pleasurably occupied in some pursuit, then it applies to every emotionally healthy adolescent. The patience and ingenuity with which young people can tinker, construct things, think up new solutions for technical problems, makes one feel that in the process of growing up both artists and inventors are lost. The young girl who in prepuberty appeared in such odd getups now turns a carefully selected remnant into an original evening dress.

Eissler (1958) emphasizes that as the solutions for inner conflicts that were devised in latency are discarded in puberty, a great deal of energy is set free. This energy is used creatively when personal conflicts are depicted in forms that apply to others as well. To this end there must be conflict as well as the potential for form-giving.

Greenacre (1957, 1958, 1959) points out that the artist becomes relatively independent of his parents quite early in life through his ability to perceive broader relationships—for example, in feeling a bond between himself and nature. In adolescence this is an extremely productive way of dealing with feelings of loneliness. Unfortunately, this often comes to an end because the adolescent is shamefaced about what he creates and experiences. Sometimes wounding remarks from those about him are responsible. These may be intended as well-meaning criticism, but the adolescent's self-esteem is so vulnerable that even objective criticism may paralyze creativity for a long time to come.

The energy that is invested in creative pursuits during adolescence is used in adulthood for the benefit of the family. Children of one's own often make "brain children" superfluous. The "love affair with the world" which to Greenacre (1957) characterizes the artist's youth, and which seems to me to exist for every emotionally healthy preschooler, must be very intense and must be supported by talent in a specific field if the creativity of adolescence is to continue into adulthood.

# 17 BASIC MISUNDERSTANDINGS BETWEEN PARENTS AND CHILDREN IN PUBERTY

What can parents do for their children in puberty, and how is the process of puberty made more difficult by parents?

Continuing from the preceding chapter, I shall begin with the second question. If parents really show no understanding of their growing children, or if they themselves show signs of intense hostility, they can give the child no significant support in his identity crisis. There is a big difference between the effect a feeling of helplessness on the part of the parents has on the child and the favorable influence exerted by tranquil parents. If either or both parents feel too great rivalry with their children or cannot tolerate their growing up in any way, if they are too preoccupied with their own sexual conflicts and their own social adaptation, the situation becomes dangerous. One must admire the young people who find within themselves the strength to cope with life even in such situations. This happens more often than one realizes, but it is certainly an unreasonable burden.

What is the support given by the parents? Certainly not in the first instance their prohibitions and their criticism, their understanding or their lack of understanding; no, it is far more a matter of their being there and of their having built up a reasonably good life together. That is what gives the pubescent confidence in the future.

In such a situation the parents may safely lack understanding and not always be able to choose the right course. The mother may still be up waiting anxiously when her son gets home at three o'clock in the morning after an interminable discussion with his friend about the deeper meaning of life, or when her daughter has been out on her first date. The pubescent will certainly resent this, but it cannot do a great deal of harm. The father may relate with exasperation how much harder he had it in his youth than boys do today, how it would never have entered his head to talk back to his father, and so on. The boy will surely resent this, but he can still regard his parents as the secure background that is so necessary in the puberty crisis.

It is not wise to meet this crisis with lack of understanding, but neither is it a serious matter. What may, however, have serious consequences is if a young person feels that he has no family background; that he cannot count on his parents in fundamental matters; that the father, not sometimes but always, disparages what the son considers important; that the mother, not sometimes but always, solicitously but without understanding continues to treat him as a little boy; that she defends her possessions against her daughter by quarreling with her on an equal footing; or that she, not sometimes but always, pokes fun at her first attempts to make herself attractive to the opposite sex.

In this period, too, a number of basic misunderstandings appear between parents and children, misunderstandings about all sorts of things, pertaining to the fact that the parents have, for good or ill, formed their views. Parents who see themselves as especially progressive discover painfully that their children look upon this particular brand of progressiveness as obsolete and stuffy. Parents who think that they have a good understanding of business problems consider their son's talk stupid and arrogant, while the son sees in his parents' talk the "establishment" from which he shies away in horror.

The most serious misunderstandings, however, appear in the sexual domain. Parents often have great difficulty in interpreting the developmental stage of their children. They have no way of knowing whether the children have sexual contact, for the children do not tell; but their fantasies about it move in one of two directions. I have heard mothers maintain very positively that their son or daughter is not remotely ready for that—while I knew from the son or daughter that he or she moved with a group in which it was customary to go in for heavy necking after the movies. Not to have had close physical contact was looked upon not only as infantile, but as reprehensible, as uncouth. The parents were, however, convinced that their children had no desire for any sexual contact because they considered it "not nice."

It is just this difference in norms between generations that makes life so bewildering for the young. At the same time these conventional norms sometimes have, for both parents and children, little to do with actual inner feelings.

The opposite fantasy also occurs quite often. The mother who sat waiting so anxiously for her son until three o'clock never for a moment imagined the interminable conversation with his friend, but pictured sexual adventures that he might be having with all the girls whose first names he had ever mentioned.

Pubescents too give evidence of this two-sided fantasy in relation to their parents. On the one hand, they cannot imagine that their parents, whom they see as old people, might have sexual relations; on the other hand, they see their parents' bedroom as the place where nothing but sex goes on.

It is particularly difficult for the child in puberty if he is confronted too directly with his parents' sexual life. This can occur if the mother has another baby during the child's puberty; it may also happen that secrets in the parents' lives are exposed, such as a concealed affair that leads to a divorce.

Let us return to the parents of the "normal" pubescent. They will discover that the criteria they used during latency to determine whether their child's development was going along well no longer serve. For several years the relationship with their child was characterized by a great deal being taken for granted. The child mostly went his own way, but counted on their affection and interest, and showed the same feelings toward them. He fitted in reasonably well at school and with friends, was dependably troublesome and lovable. If the parents did not understand the child, after a few months they found out what was wrong, or else after a little while all seemed to be well again.

During puberty none of this can any longer be considered as the norm. For the parent of a pubescent it is true that, "no matter what you do, it's wrong." Affection is seen as interference, letting alone as indifference. If one smiles kindly at dogmatic statements or at difficulties, one has no understanding of them; if one takes them up seriously, one is obviously stupid. If one withdraws from the discussion, the pubescent complains that he gets no help even from his parents.

In some cases the pubescent appears to demand a

complete reversal of roles: the parents are now to assume the child's role and to let him lay down the law to them much more severely than they have ever done. Sometimes the parents then turn away in exasperation, but that is not the wisest course. They should be able, without accepting it, to see the reversal of roles as a criterion of a normal development, albeit in an extreme form. This will also help them to retain their own identity.

The pubescent must now make his own way, sustained by whatever harmony his parents built up with him during his latency. The greater the harmony, the more smoothly the disengagement process will go. If the ties were too strong or too weak, there will be greater difficulty, and this will not be the time to reach for further contact. The problem will no doubt resolve itself when adulthood has been reached, but the bond will then be one between two independent persons.

In contrast to latency, unrest is normal in puberty, and the lack of unrest the most alarming. In adolescence this unrest will subside, and most parents will then find themselves more tranquil, too. Even so, the choice of a partner produces a considerable shock. The fact that the first child in the family brings home a girl friend or a boy friend often throws the parents into confusion. They are not conscious of wanting to keep their son or daughter tied to them, but from this point of view they see everything at its worst. On the other hand, the young people interpret their parents' honest concern about an unsatisfactory relationship as jealousy.

More often parents show too great enthusiasm; this too interferes with the adolescent's free choice. If parents take every love affair with dead seriousness and welcome

every boy or girl friend as a prospective son- or daugh-
ter-in-law, the adolescent will suffer a severe loss
of face if the affair dies out. Loss of face is very painful
for the young in their uncertainty. A light, neutral
attitude, without breaking off what the youngster may
take seriously, yet without cutting off the line of retreat,
makes development go much more smoothly. A major
advantage of young people's having apartments of their
own is that parents and children, in this final phase of the
disengagement process, are not constantly informed of
each other's doings, and the process is not disturbed by
their interaction. Once freedom has been found, the
young person feels that he can mold his own life in his
own way in his own home, free from his parents.

# 18 CONCLUSION

I have tried to describe something of the interaction between child and parents, and I have illustrated this in connection with the developmental process in the various life phases. I hope thereby to have made clear what the doctor and the educator can do to promote psychological health and what they must omit doing to avoid disturbing normal development.

Irregularities in psychological development must be neither ignored nor emphasized. The doctor should not show greater haste in referring a patient to a specialist than in the case of physical symptoms—but preferably not less. Parents are often ashamed of needing help when disturbances in their child's psychological development appear. They see the difficulties magnified in the future, and expect them to worsen. Sometimes they deny that anything is wrong, because they believe they are accountable for everything that goes wrong in their child's life. The doctor can guide them in finding the right kind of help in time without guilt. He must also understand normal development well enough to be able to reassure them about the irregularities that are part of it.

Doctors and educators who are fully aware of the many forms of active adjustment that the child makes on the road to adulthood can give the advice appropriate for a particular child and for his family. I hope, however, also to have encouraged parents to show their own warmth and resourcefulness toward the children whom they love and to whom they mean so much.

# REFERENCES

Bergmann, T. & Freud, A. (1955), *Children in the Hospital.* New York: International Universities Press.

Bladergroen, W. J. (1966), Lichamelijke en Geestelijke Ontwikkeling van Het Kind. Amsterdam: Wetenschappelijke Uitgeverij.

Blos, P. (1962), *On Adolescence.* New York: Free Press.

de Levita, D. J. (1967), Ongelukkige liefde in de adolescentie. In: *Hoofdstukken uit de Hedendaagse Psychoanalyse,* ed. P. J. van der Leeuw et al. Arnheim: van Loghum Slaterus.

Deutsch, H. (1944), *The Psychology of Women.* New York: Grune & Stratton.

Eissler, K. R. (1958), Notes on problems of technique in the psychoanalytic treatment of adolescents: with some remarks on perversions. *The Psychoanalytic Study of the Child,* 13:223-254. New York: International Universities Press.

Fenichel, O. (1945), *The Psychoanalytic Theory of Neurosis.* New York: Norton.

Fraiberg, S. H. (1965), *The Magic Years.* New York: Scribners.

Freud, A. (1958), Adolescence. *The Psychoanalytic Study of the Child,* 13:255-278. New York: International Universities Press.

_____ & Burlingham, D. (1943), *War and Children.* New York: International Universities Press, 1944.

Freud, S. (1908), Family romances. *Standard Edition,* 9:237-243. London: Hogarth Press, 1959.

_____ (1912), On the universal tendency to debasement in the sphere of love. *Standard Edition,* 11:177-190. London: Hogarth Press, 1957.

_____ (1920), Beyond the pleasure principle. *Standard Edition,* 18:3-64. London: Hogarth Press, 1955.

_____ (1929), Civilization and its discontents. *Standard Edition,* 21:59-145. London: Hogarth Press, 1961.

Fries, M. E. & Woolf, P. J. (1953), Some hypotheses on the role of the congenital activity type in personality development. *The Psychoanalytic Study of the Child,* 8:48-62. New York: International Universities Press.

Frijling-Schreuder, E. C. M. (1965a), *Preventie van neurotische Gezinsrelaties.* Assen: Van Gorcum.

_____ (1965b), Schoolziekte. *Ned. Tijdschr. voor Geneeskunde,* 109(5): 225-230.

# References

Greenacre, P. (1957), The childhood of the artist. *The Psychoanalytic Study of the Child*, 12:47-72. New York: International Universities Press.

——— (1958), The family romance of the artist. *The Psychoanalytic Study of the Child*, 13:9-43. New York: International Universities Press.

——— (1959), Play in relation to creative imagination. *The Psychoanalytic Study of the Child*, 14:61-80. New York: International Universities Press.

Hamblett, C. & Deverson, I. (1964), *Generation X*. London: Gibbs, pp. 65, 73.

Hoffer, W. (1949), Mouth, hand and ego-integration. *The Psychoanalytic Study of the Child*, 3/4:49-56. New York: International Universities Press.

Kuiper, P. C. (1966), *The Neuroses*. New York: International Universities Press, 1972.

——— Personal Communication.

Lampl-de Groot, J. (1927), The evolution of the Oedipus complex in women. In: *The Development of the Mind*. New York: International Universities Press, pp. 3-19, 1965.

——— (1950), On masturbation and its influences on general development. In: *The Development of the Mind*. New York: International Universities Press, pp. 172-198, 1965.

——— (1960), On adolescence. In: *The Development of the Mind*. New York: International Universities Press, pp. 308-317, 1965.

Mahler, M. S. in collaboration with Furer, M. (1968), *On Human Symbiosis and the Vicissitudes of Individuation*. New York: International Universities Press.

Matthews, E. (1969), Career development in girls. In: *Issues in Adolescent Psychology*, ed. D. Rogers. New York: Appleton, pp. 305-317.

Meijers, J. A. (1962), *De Taal van Het Kind*. Utrecht/Antwerp: Prisma.

Planting, G. J. (1961), *Aanleg en Ontplooiing*. Groningen: van Denderen.

Reich, A. (1960), Pathologic forms of self-esteem regulation. *The Psychoanalytic Study of the Child*, 15:215-232. New York: International Universities Press.

Salimbene, (n.d.), The Emperor Frederick II. In: *The Portable Medieval Reader*, ed. J. Ross & M. McLaughlin. New York: Viking Press, 1955, pp. 366-367.

Settlage, C. S. (1970), Adolescence and social change. *J. Amer. Acad. Child Psychiat.*, 9:203-216.

Spitz, R. A. (1957), *No and Yes*. New York: International Universities Press.

——— in collaboration with Cobliner, W. G. (1965), *The First Year of Life*. New York: International Universities Press.

van Dijk, W. K. & Hulsman, R. H. C., Eds. (1970), *Drugs in Nederland.* Bussum: Paul Brand.

Whiting, J. W. M. & Child, I. L. (1953), *Child Training and Personality. A Cross-Cultural Study.* New Haven: Yale University Press.

Wolff, P. H. (1969), The natural history of crying and other vocalizations in early infancy. In: *Determinants of Infant Behavior,* 4, ed. B. M. Foss. London: Methuen, pp. 81-109.